THE END OF THE LINE?

The End of the Line?

*The Development of Christian Theology
in the Last Two Centuries*

John H. S. Kent

SCM PRESS LTD

First published under the title 'Christian Theology in the
Eighteenth to the Twentieth Centuries', being the final
chapter in the volume *A History of Christian Doctrine*
edited by Hubert Cunliffe-Jones, T. & T. Clark 1978. This
edition published by arrangement.

334 00383 0

This edition first published 1982
by SCM Press Ltd
58 Bloomsbury Street London WC1B 3QX

Printed in Great Britain by
Richard Clay (The Chaucer Press) Ltd,
Bungay, Suffolk

Contents

Introduction:
The End of the Line?

For the beginning is assuredly
the end – since we know nothing, pure
and simple, beyond
our own complexities.
Paterson, by William Carlos Williams

Christianity began as a religion of certainties. God had intervened in history and had established his own unique, absolute self-revelation, localized in the Bible, broadcast in the church. Not only had God expressed himself perfectly through Jesus, but he continued to act in the history of individuals, peoples, states and religious institutions. Nothing symbolizes this tradition better than the view that God did not leave us at the mercy of our own misunderstanding of the Gospels (for we were bound to misinterpret them) but provided an organ of ecclesiastical infallibility to which we could turn in matters of faith and morals for utterly trustworthy decisions. Nor does anything suggest more clearly the extent to which modern Protestantism has failed to develop beyond its sixteenth-century origins than the way in which its ecumenical leaders try to incorporate the idea of infallibility into their theology of a united ecclesia. Whether you take your stand at the end or the beginning of the line of Christian history, you find a similar emphasis on Christianity as knowledge (in the sense that 'knowledge' can be taught in schools with authority, and indeed ought to be), and on the availability of divine power to change historical situations and individual lives.

The twentieth century, on the other hand, would hardly by itself have been the obvious breeding-ground for such ideas. The underlying mood of the modern period can be found in Nietzsche, in *Twilight of the Idols* (1889) for example, in a passage like this: 'No one is accountable for existing at all, or for being constituted as he is, or for living in the circumstances and surroundings in which he lives . . . He is *not* the result of a special design, a will, a purpose; he is *not* the subject of an attempt to attain to an "ideal of man" or an "ideal of happiness" or "an ideal of morality" – it is absurd to want to hand over his nature to some purpose or other. We invented the concept "purpose": in reality purpose is *lacking* . . . That no one is any longer made accountable – *this alone is the great liberation* – thus alone is the innocence of becoming restored . . .' There is no such thing as purpose – we invented purpose: whatever the driving theory of historical action – Christian, Marxist, nationalist, Western humanist – we invented the theories and are answerable to none of them. The disillusioned historian can no longer write off the accumulating cruelty of the century to experience, or education, or free will, or 'the helplessness of God'. Freed from the pressure to find in history a special design, or will, or purpose, or even sense, the historian recognizes that there is no built-in safeguard in the system which will prevent men from fulfilling their foulest hopes. It is as though humanity were shedding its biological instinct for self-preservation and over-adapting to the chance of self-destruction. One senses the end of a line of growth, an end which neither Marxism nor Christianity can prevent, not even when they combine in 'liberation theology', which would like to see itself as legitimizing an ecclesiastical take-over of a post-revolutionary situation, but which may be more correctly interpreted as a theology of nostalgia – the characteristic theology of the twentieth century – a harking back to the style of the *ancien régime*, however paradoxical this may sound, to a society in which the churches regarded themselves as the spiritual form of a material community. If the politics of the present century simply reflect human appetite – and I don't believe for a moment that they do more – no human interest of survival will be served by committing what remains of the Christian tradition to politics in any of its twentieth-century forms. A theology of survival would be more to the point than a theology of liberation. Survival, however, is a political issue, and we shall depend much more upon diplomacy than on ideological crusades.

Such speculations raise the question of how near Christianity itself has come to the end of its own line. Religion as such, of course, seems less at risk than Christianity, because religion does not need an elaborate system of doctrine as a survival-kit. A Western theist, for example, might be satisfied, without any question of certainty, with the belief that the universe is ultimately intelligible and morally at least bearable: one could endure, if not enjoy, life. He would not be at all obliged to defend the possibility of miracle, or of divine intervention in the history of individuals or races. He might well accept the view, which I hold myself, that all religious, and especially Christian statements, like scientific theories, are hypothetical – are thrown out in our constant struggle to master our brief living experience of a largely incomprehensible universe. William James, who was his own kind of theist, said that it was a mistake to hold any opinion as though it never could be reinterpretable or corrigible. But radical empiricism, as he named it, ought equally not to inhibit action: hypotheses should be tested, as well as held. Orthodox doctrines of the Trinity, the divinity of Christ, the atonement as some kind of satisfaction for human sin, seem more useful as hypotheses about the New Testament than they do as hypotheses about twentieth-century life, and they are more easily tested in terms of the text of those documents than in any other way. Unfortunately, another feature of the modern history of Christian thought has been the steady decline in the authority of the New Testament as an adequate ground for absolute certainty in religion. The relationship between the New Testament and modern Christianity may be summed up in a story told by the famous Jewish writer, S. J. Agnon, and quoted by the equally great Jewish scholar, Gershom Sholem, in his book, *Major Trends in Jewish Mysticism*:

> When the Baal Shem had a difficult task before him, he would go to a certain place in the woods, light a fire and meditate in prayer – and what he had set out to perform was done. When a generation later the 'Maggid'

of Mcseritz was faced with the same task he would go to the same place
in the woods and say: We can no longer light the fire, but we can still
speak the prayers – and what he wanted done became reality. Again a
generation later Rabbi Moshe Lieb of Sassov had to perform this task.
And he too went into the woods and said: We can no longer light a fire,
nor do we know the secret meditations belonging to the prayer, but we do
know the place in the woods to which it all belongs – and that must be
sufficient – and sufficient it was. But when another generation had passed
and Rabbi Israel of Rishin was called upon to perform the task, he sat
down on his golden chair in his castle and said: We cannot light the fire,
we cannot speak the prayers, we do not know the place, but we can tell
the story of how it was done. And, the story-teller adds, the story which
he told had the same effect as the actions of the other three.

In its original context, this story symbolizes the decline of Jewish
mysticism in eastern Europe in the eighteenth century, but the same story
applies to the Christian case. We can no longer be sure that we are in touch
with the original meaning of the central stories of the Gospels. We can only
tell the stories; we cannot really judge their effect. In fact, it is not just a
question of whether we can 'understand' stories which are receding steadily
into a lost world of the past, but whether we can go on believing – as we
have to do if this is to be a case of revelation – that the stories are protean
enough to communicate to twentieth-century readers lost in a maze which
changes all the time, and in ever more terrifying ways. The survival of any
religious system depends upon the power of its images to renew themselves,
and the study of modern historical theology which I have attempted here
suggests that if Christianity is nearing the end of its main, public line, this
is because it has exhausted ways of keeping its images alive. More than
seventy years ago the Catholic lay theologian, Friedrich von Hügel, was
lamenting that the ideas of original sin and judgment had ceased to
stimulate people to detachment and otherworldliness: science (he thought)
was now the best way of purgation available, a discipline of self-denying,
disinterested, long-drawn-out enquiry which would, for those who could
stand the strain, work for purgation. That at least seems sounder than
supposing – as some present-day religious writers seem to suppose – that
dogma can somehow be saved as the largely unexamined residue of feeling
left at the end of a performance of the liturgy, as though one could simply
say that we *know* that Christ was present in the eucharist. And without a
firmer structure than this, religion becomes the raw material of more
powerful emotional states, such as nationalism, as we have seen both in
Northern Ireland and in Iran in recent years. The modern state has cut
loose from civilization at the very moment when effective self-restraint in
the use of power has become vital to human survival on the planet. The
images of power in the New Testament – at any rate in the Gospels – are
unambiguous enough to be of no service to the state, but little has been made
of them in modern theology. And there is no sign that primitive Christianity repudiated the chance of political power once it was able to lay its hands
on it.

Does this imply that I feel, in the first place, that all that the critical
theology of the last two hundred years has achieved is to show how little
we can say about God with any kind of certainty at all; and, in the second
place, that the increasingly destructive trail of human behaviour over the
same period has finally demolished the old Christian case for a God who
intervened not only in Jesus but in the history of individuals, of states, of
the 'church' itself? Are we not only at the end of the line, but also at a point
of no return?

I doubt that the position of the religious thinker is so hopeless. However
much he feels that his personality is being dissolved into a society which
has momentum without direction, he can still use inherent psychological
capacity to halt the unenlightening flow of events by bringing his own
existence into the forefront of his own consciousness, so as to contemplate
his own birth and death. To quote Nietzsche again:

> It is always as in the last moment before the departure of an emigrant-
> ship; people have more than ever to say to one another, the hour
> presses, the ocean with its lonely silence waits impatiently behind all
> the noise . . . And all, all suppose that the past has been nothing or a
> small matter, that the future is everything: hence this haste, this
> crying, this self-deafening and self-overreaching. Everyone wants to be
> foremost in his future – and yet death and the stillness of death are the
> only things certain and common to all in this future.

Nietzsche himself wanted to combine this tragic sense of existence with
a passionate affirmation of the creativity of man, however fragile and soon
misunderstood. For the critical theologian, for the Christian humanist, the
assertion of belief, of belief in God, in human creativity, in the Gospels
as one sign of that human capacity to make peace instead of a desert, is now
more than ever a matter of faith: faith in the underlying rationality of the
universe, which the traditional Christian cosmology, alas, does not encour-
age; faith in the quality of life commended in what seems to have been the
teaching of Jesus – rather than in the pronouncements of ecclesiastics too
easily influenced by social pressures (and pressure-groups); faith in reason,
however unfashionable reason may have become in the sick romanticism of
today.

> Like a doctor prescribing a medicine for each disease
> I use whatever remedy is at hand to save the world.
> (*Cold Mountain*, 100 Poems by the T'ang poet, Han-Shan,
> translated by Burton Watson.)

I

THE EIGHTEENTH CENTURY

The history of theology between 1760 and 1960 can without undue distortion be treated as a whole. It was a period in which the classical theologies of Catholicism and Protestantism (which this book has already described) had to fight for life against wave after wave of criticism from both inside and outside organized Christianity. To some extent this intellectual struggle followed its own inner logic: social and political change could not obliterate what Hume and Kant said, for example, so that even in the mid-twentieth century a hostile discussion of the case for Christian theism (in Anthony Flew's *God and Philosophy*, 1966, for instance) was still dominated by their arguments. Theology was also affected by sociological change, however, by the development of a mass, technological, urban society in which scientific progress seemed to confirm a rejection of the belief in the supernatural which had already taken place for the sophisticated in the eighteenth century.

This combination of social and intellectual change drove Christianity from the centre to somewhere near the margin of western society, a change symbolized in the way in which in the modern university Christian theology has become a minority subject, or a component part of 'the study of religion'. As for those who still retained their belief in the fixed dogmatic orthodoxy of the past, they saw themselves faced with the problem of how to restore the Church's past ascendancy in western society without compromising theological traditions which they had inherited. Another, more critical school of theologians became convinced that the intellectual and social changes were so far-reaching that they necessitated a theological transformation of Christianity. It was the widespread feeling that what was becoming a post-Christian society no longer accepted the claim of the Churches to possess an immutable, clearly defined body of revealed religious knowledge about both God and Man – the kind of theology which was summarized for the Reformed tradition, for instance in the *Compendium of Christian Theology* which Johannes Wollebius (1586–1629) published in 1626 – which gave a peculiar edge to the nineteenth-century controversies between orthodoxy and 'liberalism'. The stage had been set, however, in the previous century when the Church had failed as a whole to anticipate the impending collapse of the traditional social order and remained committed to the customary centres of power. Complacent Roman Catholic support for the crumbling French absolute monarchy, and an equally worldly Anglican involvement in the fortunes of the Hanoverian dynasty

symbolized this failure and helped to fix the Enlightenment in an anti-
Christian position. In Germany, Protestant religious institutions enjoyed a
similar cultural prestige and also identified themselves with the *ancien
régime*, a fact which is explicable if one accepts that, as Ernst Troeltsch
maintained, the Protestant Reformation was not so much an expression of
the beginnings of the 'modern spirit' as a movement strictly within the
intellectual limits of medieval culture. Classical Protestantism flourished
between 1517 and the end of the seventeenth century, but went into decline
after 1700 and must be distinguished from the kind of Protestantism which
then developed in association with the rationalist mood of the Enlightenment, as well as from the liberal Protestantism of the nineteenth century.
In the eighteenth century the social function of theology – which is to
provide a system of explanations and actions (or rituals) which will give
meaning to life as a whole for the individual and also help to solidify a
specific society – was being steadily eroded because the society itself was
ceasing to hold the allegiance of some of the ablest men it produced. One
cannot continue to pay social homage to religion in the sceptical style
familiarized by Montaigne if one no longer believes in the value of the social
system whose stability is to some extent reinforced by common religious
practices and explanations. If one wants instead to destroy the social order,
the religion which helps to bind it together becomes a part of the target.
For a society which does not value itself, religion cannot exist on the
strength of its alleged value to society. In the mid-twentieth century, when
the situation has become more acute, some Christian theologians have
reacted by demanding a theology of 'revolution', or a 'political' theology
(as Harvey Cox, the author of *The Secular City* (1965), would call it), but
most eighteenth-century theologians defended both the theological and the
social past. As a result, they did not dominate the thought of the period:
the British Deists, the French *philosophes* and the writers of the German
Enlightenment like Reimarus and Lessing felt it necessary to attack both
Christian institutions and Christian doctrine, and in doing so threw the
theologians even more on to the defensive, so that the best-known English
theological work of the period, Bishop Butler's *Analogy of Religion* (1736),
was primarily composed as a reply to the Deists.

Various factors helped to change the intellectual climate of theological
thought in the seventeenth and eighteenth centuries. Among them were
geographical discovery, which meant contact with non-European cultures,
the scientific discoveries of Isaac Newton, and the effect on the humanist
tradition of the long series of 'wars of religion' and of the divisions of the
western Church. Christian historiography has always exaggerated the
decisiveness for the history of theology of the Reformation and Counter-
Reformation, and has passed swiftly over the period between 1550 and
1700; but it was in these later years that the split in European culture
became acute. This culture, which had never been completely unified in the
medieval period on either a Classical or a Christian basis, began to fall
radically apart during the sixteenth century, a process which the successive
waves of Protestant and Roman Catholic religious renewal did little to
check. The degree of religious doubt latent in Renaissance humanists like

the Italian philosopher, Pomponazzi, is a matter of some dispute: one scholar has said that 'in the light of his passionate and consistent advocacy of a purely secular and this-worldly morality, as well as of his insistence in the *Apologia*, the *Defensorium* and the *De Nutritione*, that immortality is contrary to all the principles of natural reason, it remains a moot question how seriously he took his contention that immortality is nevertheless a "religious truth" ' (cf. *The Renaissance Philosophy of Man*. ed. E. Cassirer, 1959, p. 18). By the end of the sixteenth century, in any case, the sceptical tradition had established itself as an independent element in the cultural pattern, and it is significant that the most important source-book of the English Deists, Lord Edward Herbert's *De Veritate*, was published as early as 1624. Herbert (1583–1648) had little influence in his troubled life-time, but his assertion that God had, quite apart from Christianity, revealed to all men what was necessary for salvation, stood in sharp contrast to the bitter division between Laudian and Puritan which was one of the causes of what was not only a secular but also England's 'religious war'.

In general, the Churches were able to invoke the authority of the State to ban or censor direct attacks on Christianity itself, but the development of a religious alternative to Christianity – for this was what early eighteenth-century Deism set out to be – could only be delayed, not stopped. John Locke's *Reasonableness of Christianity as delivered in the Scriptures* (1695) was an attempt to reconcile the Christian claim to a direct divine revelation in the Bible with the kind of simple ethical theism which Lord Herbert had codified for his successors; it is also important as an example of the reduced sort of Christianity which was to appear again and again in the liberal tradition, a tradition which accepted the strength of the critical, rationalist attitude which had been developing since the Renaissance, but which clung with determination and even sometimes with passion to the value of the Christian religious tradition. In his essay on 'liberalism' in the *Apologia pro Sua Vita* (1865) John Henry Newman called it the 'Anti-Dogmatic Principle', and said that religious liberalism started from the mistake of subjecting to human judgment those revealed doctrines which in their very nature were beyond and independent of it, and of claiming to determine on intrinsic grounds the truth and value of propositions which rested for their reception simply on the external authority of the divine Word. It would certainly be fair to describe the kind of religious rationalism which Newman was attacking as at any rate 'non-dogmatic', for one of the enduring characteristics of the school was its comparative indifference to dogmatic orthodoxy, and especially to the doctrines of original sin (which John Locke, for instance, claimed to be unable to find in the Scriptures), the atonement (in most of its classical interpretations), eternal punishment (which Locke, once again, dispensed with), the sacraments, and the Church, a body which non-dogmatic liberals usually disliked, partly because religious institutions were often intolerant of doctrinal variation, and partly because institutionalized Christianity sometimes seemed more concerned with temporal than spiritual power. Ernst Cassirer (in *The Philosophy of the Enlightenment*, E.T., 1951) regarded as a fundamental principle of the Enlightenment the view that it was dogma and not doubt which was the

true enemy of morality and religion; the non-dogmatic liberals carried this
attitude over into the nineteenth century, strengthened by the anti-
metaphysical influence of Kant.

The liberal tradition had other characteristics, however, to which
Newman did not sufficiently refer, expecially that of Christocentricism –
understood as an emphasis on the central rôle of the Jesus of the Gospels
not only as a religious leader and teacher but also as the living source of an
immediate freedom. Jesus was the justification of Liberal tolerance. One
should be cautious, moreover, of accepting the assertion, still often made,
that nineteenth-century Protestant Liberalism mainly developed as a
response to the advances of natural science. The influence of nineteenth-
century scientific method was confirmatory rather than primary; it sprang
from and confirmed the value of the rationalist tradition, and produced the
sort of results which rationalist theologians had anticipated, not in detail,
but in general. This has been obscured in Britain by the immense controversy which surrounded the publication of Charles Darwin's *Origin of
Species* in 1859. It was certainly true, as Paul Tillich said (in *Perspectives on
19th and 20th century Protestant Theology*. 1967) that after 1859 'Christian
theology was like an army retreating in the face of another advancing army.
With every new breakthrough of the advancing army Christian theology
would attempt to protect the Christian tradition' [which here meant, of
course, what we have called dogmatic orthodoxy] 'which still remained
untouched. Then a new breakthrough would make the previous defence
untenable, and so another retreat and setting up of a new defence would be
necessary' (p. 158).

But it was dogmatic orthodoxy which retreated in the second half of the
nineteenth century. Armed with its own, earlier rationalism, and with its
immediate, undogmatic reliance upon the spirit of the living Jesus, Protestant Liberalism had not so much to retreat as to hold on to positions
which theologians like Schleiermacher had established in the earlier part of
the century. Even Albrecht Ritschl (1822–89), whose liberalism was
certainly less than his Lutheranism, understood what was at stake, and
wrote that 'in every religion what is sought, with the help of the super-
human spiritual power reverenced by man, is a solution of the contradiction
in which man finds himself as both a part of the world of nature and a
spiritual personality claiming to dominate nature. For in the former rôle he
is a part of nature, dependent upon her, subject to and confined by other
things; but as spirit he is moved by the impulse to maintain his independence against them. In this juncture, religion springs up as a faith in super-
human spiritual powers, by whose help the power which man possesses of
himself is in some way supplemented and elevated into a unity of its own
kind which is a match for the pressure of the natural world' (*Justification
and Reconciliation*, iii, 1888, p. 199). Whatever else Ritschl meant by this –
and he certainly did not exaggerate the extent to which the Christian could
know that he was being supplemented and elevated by supernatural
spiritual powers – he did not mean that a post-Kantian Christianity had to
beat a retreat in the face of the advances of natural science.

From this point of view John Locke's *Reasonableness of Christianity* pointed towards the future. Locke tried to go behind the Biblical and dogmatic controversies which had divided seventeenth-century Christendom, and to read the Bible without the prejudices of either the Roman Catholic or classical Protestant theological systems, to take, as he claimed, 'the plain, direct meaning of words and phrases' (p.2). Read in this common-sense fashion the Scriptures seemed to add to, rather than contradict, Lord Herbert's 'natural religion' as to what was essential to salvation: men had to repent and acknowledge that Jesus was the Messiah; God would regard this faith as making up for the believer's failure to achieve moral perfection. Christ's significance in the history of religion was that his divine authority (which Locke in this essay established on the orthodox basis of his fulfilment of Old Testament prophecies and by his working of the miracles recorded in the New Testament) freed men from the polytheism and idolatry and perverted religious ritual of the past; Jesus assured men that the moral order was guaranteed by God and promised them that they might expect divine assistance in their attempts to behave well. It was Christ, so to speak, who first showed men what the true form of religion was, and it was his supernatural authority to do this which men were really acknowledging when they declared their faith in him as the Messiah. Like many later rationalist theologians, however, Locke was not prepared to commit himself to the proposition that faith in Jesus as the Messiah was necessary to salvation. In any case Locke rejected the classical context of the traditional doctrine of salvation in as much as he abandoned the ideas of original sin and eternal punishment.

Giving a guarded assent to the possibility that the Christian revelation offered a kind of divine supplement to or a confirmation of the religious insights obtained by human reason, Locke produced a reduced but recognizable Christianity. The principal Deist writers, however, wanted to replace Christianity, not to reform it; and the attack which John Toland (1670–1722) may be said to have started when at the age of twenty-six he published *Christianity not Mysterious* (1696) continued to spread throughout Europe for the remainder of the eighteenth century. It is inaccurate to speak of Deism as in decline by about 1730, or to suggest that Bishop Butler (by an appeal to reason) and John Wesley (by an appeal to religious experience) somehow obliterated the very memory of the Deist position. Toland exalted reason above revelation, which Locke had not done, and dismissed from Christianity all suggestions of mystery and miracle, as well as dogmas like that of the Trinity, which he said were unintelligible. Samuel Clarke (in *A Discourse concerning the Unchangeable Obligations of Natural Religion*, 1711) renewed the appeal to the knowledge of right religion which was held to be the possession of every man born into the world. Anthony Collins (1676–1729) criticized the traditional argument that Jesus proved his claim to be the Messiah by the fulfilment of Old Testament prophecies (see, for instance, his *Discourse of the Grounds and Reasons of the Christian Religion*, 1724). Matthew Tindal (in *Christianity as Old as the Creation*, 1730) objected to the Christian picture of God on moral grounds; Christianity had only perverted a natural religion which was old as the creation of man. A later powerful contribution to the Deist position was Conyers Middleton's *Free Inquiry into the Miraculous Powers which are supposed to have subsisted in the Christian Church* (1749).

The traditional picture of Deism has not been adequately revised since Leslie Stephen wrote his *History of English Thought in the Eighteenth Century* (1876). The Deist attack was not important as part of Christian theology itself, but as a vital part of the context within which Christian theology had to operate after 1700. Orthodox historians ignore the revolutionary nature of the Deist movement and emphasize instead the violence of its controversial methods – without seeing that these reflect the Deist sense of being a handful of Lilliputians in arms against a race of Gullivers. Orthodox church historians still stress the weaknesses of Deism, 'its lack of historical insight, its blindness to the power of evil, its tone of supercilious superiority, its consistent silence about Jesus Christ' (*Reason and Authority in the Eighteenth Century*, G. R. Cragg, 1964, p. 69). They miss the origin of the mood that inspired the Deists, their horror at what they felt to be the inadequacy of classical Protestantism with its emphasis on the supernatural, its morally questionable doctrines of the atonement, its lack of interest in the fate of those born outside the historical Christian community, its insistence on relating morality, of which the Deists approved, to beliefs which they regarded as a mass of superstition. The orthodox were shocked at the satirical vigour with which writers like Collins treated the Bible; they did not understand how the Bible itself shocked the Deists. They did not share the Deist feeling that classical Christian theology contradicted what Isaac Newton and other scientists were revealing about the true nature of God, who must have ensured that all men had an equal opportunity of knowing how he wanted them to live. It was a kind of rationalist and moral contempt which made Collins so biting in his attacks. The Tindal of 1730 apart, the Deists were young men in revolt: their stylistic ancestor was the Erasmus of such colloquies as *The Shipwreck*. (Erasmus' *Colloquies* were translated by Roger L'Estrange at the end of the seventeenth century, and again by N. Bailey in 1725). Once one sees that the Deists belong to the history of European religion rather than to the history of Christianity, one sees that it was no particular criticism of their religious sincerity to say that they were anti-Christian.

More relevant perhaps was the fact that the Deist campaign to discredit the alleged divine authority of the Christian Scriptures was not entirely unsuccessful. 'After the Deists it was far more difficult to treat Holy Writ as a simple, clear and unequivocal doctrinal authority. Its ambiguities and discrepancies had been probed into, some of its ethical crudities (especially in the Old Testment) had been exposed, and the twin pillars of the Evidences – prophecies and miracles – were already seen by a percipient few to be as much stumbling blocks as stepping stones to faith . . . Thus John Conybeare's *Scripture Difficulties Considered* (1732) allowed that the Bible contained many puzzling "darknesses", many apparent contradictions still unresolved by human scholarship. Francis Webber's *Jewish Dispensations Considered* (1737) ended on a note of near defeatism, remarking that "the difficulties which attend the Scriptures of the Old Testament are not insuperable". How many churchmen felt in moments of secret doubt what Conyers Middleton openly admitted, that it was no longer possible to maintain "that every single passage of Scripture . . . must needs be received as the very word and as the voice of God himself".' (J. Walsh, *Essays in Modern Church History* ed. Bennett and Walsh, 1966, p. 150; the quotation is from Middleton, *A Letter to Dr. Waterland*, 1731, pp. 44f.)

Locke and the Deists shared the conviction that religious knowledge consisted of (a) a number of propositions about God (which Locke, of course, was more willing to derive from the Scriptures than were the Deists) and (b) what may be called moral experience. The Deists accepted the summary of 'natural religion' arrived at by Lord Herbert, that God existed and ought to be worshipped; that the sincerest form of worship was virtuous behaviour – a view which Immanuel Kant reaffirmed powerfully at the close of the eighteenth century; that men ought to repent of their wrong-doing; and that God would allot rewards and punishments to men in a future life. The only religious 'experience' in their sense was moral experience, and Bishop Butler, for that matter, was taking a similar line when he criticized the religious revivalists. George Whitefield and John Wesley, for what he called 'pretending to extraordinary sayings and communications of the Holy Ghost': Butler was afraid that this new outburst of popular religion, which emphasized special providences and 'leadings' and 'promptings' of the Spirit, would lay the Church more open to the Deist contention that Christianity was full of irrational superstition.

This did not mean that the dogmatic orthodoxy which Butler was defending did not allow for the possibility of man's being capable not only of moral experience but also of a direct, sensible experience of God; but this capacity was carefully defined as God's freedom to invade the human personality and not as man's freedom to reach out and attain knowledge of the divine personality. The credibility, nature and value of alleged 'religious experiences' was often debated in the eighteenth century, one of the most interesting discussions being in the works of the American Calvinist theologian and philosopher of religion, Jonathan Edwards (1703–58), not least in his *Inquiry into the Modern Prevailing Notions concerning that Freedom of the Will which is supposed to be Necessary to Moral Agency* (1754). For Edwards, man was not free but preserved from self-destruction through sin only by the merciful will of God, who might at any time righteously withdraw his mercy allowing the sinner to fall, not into annihilation, but into fire. Edwards was a remarkable case, because whereas in an early book, *A Faithful Narrative of the Surprising Works of God* (1737), in which he gave an account of the religious revival which had followed his own evocative preaching in Northampton, Massachusetts, he tried to describe and analyse conversion as a variety of religious experience, he came in later years, as may be gathered from his treatise *On the Religious Affections* (1746), to doubt the validity of almost every kind of religious experience found in a typical religious revival, on the ground that it was almost impossible to distinguish significant from assumed symptoms. He seems to have been gradually driven to the conclusion that genuine and significant conversion was rare, an event to be associated with a particular kind of individual who was able to be radically changed by God. The mid-

eighteenth-century religious revivals which characterized the Methodist
movement involved John Wesley in similar discussions, but Wesley showed
less analytical power than Edwards, and a greater willingness to accept his
followers' religious experience without question.

This controversy about the possibility of human religious experience in
a Christian sense (together with the controversy about the authority of the
Bible), remained the fundamental question for the future of Christianity
throughout our period. Schleiermacher, Soeren Kierkegaard, J. H. Newman,
F. D. Maurice, von Hügel, and even paradoxically, Dietrich Bonhoeffer, all
sought to protect Christianity against what they took to be the damaging
assaults of the Enlightenment by establishing the rights, the validity of the
kind of statement which John Baillie, for example, was still making in *Our
Knowledge of God* in 1939: 'It is not as the result of an inference of any kind
. . . that the knowledge of God's reality comes to us. It comes through our
direct personal encounter with him in the Person of Jesus Christ his Son our
Lord' (p. 143). This is the normal, orthodox assertion. For a modern version
of the eighteenth-century criticisms of it one may compare *God and the
Philosophers* (1966) by Anthony Flew. He was perhaps too easily satisfied
with the argument that it is impossible to make direct and self-authenticating inferences from the character of subjective experience to conclusions
about the supposedly corresponding objective facts. Theologians, on the
other hand, have frequently been satisfied with very loose statements about
our 'encounter with God'. Another acute criticism of the notion of a self-
authenticating 'encounter' with God may be found in Ronald Hepburn's
Christianity and Paradox (1958).

John Locke's formulation of the difficulties of such theological statements
characterized one side of eighteenth-century opinion. It is to be found in
chapter nineteen of the fourth book of *The Essay on the Human Understanding*, where Locke, having distinguished between faith and reason as
grounds of assent, went on to speak of enthusiasm, or direct religious
experience of God 'which, laying by reason, would set up revelation without
it. Whereby in effect it takes away both reason and revelation and substi-
tutes in the room of it the ungrounded fancies of a man's own brain, and
subsumes them for a foundation of both opinion and conduct . . . Immediate
revelation being a much easier way for men to establish their opinions and
regulate their conduct than the tedious and not always successful labour of
strict reasoning, it is no wonder that some have been very apt to pretend to
revelation and to persuade themselves that they are under the peculiar
guidance of Heaven in their actions and opinions . . . God, I own, cannot be
denied to be able to enlighten the understanding by a ray darted into the
mind immediately from the fountain of light; this they understand he has
promised to do, and who then has so good a title to expect it as those who
are his peculiar people, chosen by him and depending on him?' Such men,
Locke said, 'see the light infused into their understanding and cannot be
mistaken . . . they feel the hand of God moving them within, and the
impulses of the Spirit, and cannot be mistaken in what they feel. But here,
let me ask: this seeing, is it the perception of the truth of the proposition,
or of this, that it is a revelation from God? . . . The question then here is,

how do I know that God is the revealer of this to me; that this impression is made on my mind by the Holy Spirit? If I do not know this, how great soever the assurance is that I am possessed with, it is groundless, it is but enthusiasm . . . But how shall it be known that any proposition in our minds is a truth infused by God . . .? Here it is that enthusiasm fails of the evidence it pretends to. . . . The strength of our persuasions is no evidence at all of their rectitude. . . . If this internal light, or any proposition that under that title we take for inspired, be conformable to the principles of reason, or to the Word of God, which is attested revelation, reason warrants it and we may safely receive it for true, and be guided by it in our belief and actions: if it receive no testimony from either of these rules, we cannot take it for revelation, or for so much as true, till we have other mark that it is a revelation besides our believing it so. Thus we see the holy men of old, who had revelations from God, had something else besides that internal light of assurance in their own minds.' Moses, for instance, had the burning bush. 'It is not the strength of our private persuasion within ourselves that can warrant it to be a light or motion from God; nothing can do that but the written word of God without us, or that standard of reason which is common to us with all men.'

In the long run this line of argument culminated in the conclusion which Professor Flew, for example, formulated when he said that since the epistemological question (i.e. how do I know that God is addressing me directly?) is inescapable, 'and if, as everyone agrees, it cannot be met by reference to immediate observation or other common-place tests – then the whole argument from religious experience must collapse into an argument from whatever other credentials may be offered to authenticate the revelation supposedly mediated by such experience' (p. 139). Here the emotive word 'collapse' seems too strong: it is not impossible, for instance, to invoke the history of Christian sanctity (as von Hügel did) to support an assertion of the reality of God's existence.

For the other side of the argument in the eighteenth century one must turn to Bishop Butler (1692 1752), the ablest defender of orthodoxy and the author of *The Analogy of Religion, Natural and Revealed, to the Constitution and Course of Nature* (1736). In general, Butler opposed the Deists by emphasizing the limits of human reason: thus, just as men could not understand more than a small part of the working of nature, so they must admit that Christianity was a scheme quite beyond their comprehension as a whole, and one which they were not competent to criticize on the ground that it was not the kind of revelation, in form or content, that they would either have expected or preferred. On this ground, Butler advanced his general defence of the authority of the Bible:

'And thus we see, that the only question concerning the truth of Christianity is, whether it be a real revelation: not whether it be attended with every circumstance which we should have looked for; and concerning the authority of the Scripture, whether it be what it claims to be: not whether it be a book of such a sort and so promulgated as weak men are apt to fancy a book containing a divine revelation should. And therefore neither obscurity nor seeming inaccuracy of style, nor various readings nor early

disputes about the authors of particular parts; nor any other things of the
like kind, though they had been much more considerable in degree than
they are, could overthrow the authority of the Scripture: unless the
Prophets, Apostles, or our Lord, had promised that the book containing the
Divine revelation should be secure from those things. Nor indeed can any
objections overthrow such a kind of revelation as the Christian claims to be,
since there are no objections to the morality of it, but such as can shew, that
there is no proof of miracles wrought originally in attestation of it; no
appearance of anything miraculous in its obtaining in the world; nor any
of prophecy, that is, of events foretold, which human sagacity could not
foresee. If it can be shewn, that the proof alleged for all these is absolutely
none at all, then is revelation overturned. But were it allowed, that the
proof of any one or all of them is lower than is allowed; yet, whilst any
proof of them remains, revelation will stand upon much the same foot as it
does at present as to all the purposes of life and practice.' (*Analogy*, Pt. 11,
ch. 3, p. 185, ed. 1874.)

Here the question of 'moral' objections to Christianity referred to the
question as to whether the Scripture contained things 'plainly contradictory
to wisdom, justice or goodness; to what the light of nature teaches us of
God' (*ib.* p. 193). In the *Analogy* (pt. 11, ch. 5) Butler considered and
dismissed moral objections to the interpretation of Christ's death as offering
a vicarious satisfaction for sin, objections which, as far as Protestantism
was concerned, might be traced behind the Deist writers to late sixteenth-
century Socinianism. He took as an example the view that the doctrine of
Christ's being appointed to suffer for the sins of the world represented God
as being indifferent whether he punished the innocent or the guilty. 'The
world,' Butler replied, 'is a constitution or system whose parts have a
mutual reference to each other: and there is a scheme of things gradually
carrying on, called the course of nature, to the carrying on of which God
has appointed us in various ways to contribute. And when, in the daily
course of natural providence, it is appointed that innocent people should
suffer for the faults of the guilty, this is liable to the very same objection
we are now considering' (p. 223). In other words, this objection to the idea
of vicarious satisfaction applied as much to the whole scheme of Theism and
the whole notion of Religion as against Christianity, and could not therefore
be safely used by the Deist writers as a criticism of the Christian system.
Butler described Christ's death as both a 'satisfaction' and as 'a propitiatory
sacrifice', but he left the terms undefined, adding that in any case 'we seem
to be very much in the dark concerning the manner in which the ancients
understood atonement to be made, i.e. pardon to be obtained by sacrifices'
(*ib.* p. 221). He rejected the Deist view that human repentance sufficed by
itself to save men from future punishment (*ib.* p. 212). That the world was
in a state of ruin Butler held to be 'a supposition which seems the very
ground of the Christian dispensation, and which, if not proveable by reason,
yet is in no wise contrary to it (*ib.* p. 213). God, however, had mercifully
provided that there should be an interposition to prevent the destruction of
mankind, which men were themselves powerless to prevent, with or without
repentance. God did this through the gift of his son, 'who interposed in such

a manner as was necessary and effectual to prevent that execution of justice upon sinners which God had appointed should otherwise have been executed upon them' (*ib.* p. 214). At this point Butler was less obviously throwing light on the orthodox doctrine of the work of Christ than putting down a smoke-screen to obscure the cruder features of the position. His account differed sharply from the ideas of Locke and the Deists and was hardly likely to have impressed those in the rationalist tradition.

As for the miraculous, Butler argued that 'the extraordinary phenomena of nature' – he instanced electricity and magnetism – suggested that there could be no presumption against miracles which rendered them in any way incredible. Moreover, though a man might say that the historical evidence for miracles wrought in attestation of Christianity was not sufficient to convince him that they had happened, he could not deny that historical evidence existed. In the case of the argument from prophecy, Butler asserted that although his opponents might claim that the conformity between the prophecies and events was accidental, there were many instances in which the conformity itself could not be denied. It followed that both prophecy and miracle could still be invoked as evidence of the divine authority of the Christian revelation.

The argument from prophecy fell rapidly into the background as Biblical criticism developed in the nineteenth century. Nevertheless, Butler's position was still echoed as recently as 1938 in the official Report on *Doctrine in the Church of England*, a document which offered a fair summary of orthodoxy after the First World War, and which was produced by a committee whose chairman was William Temple. 'In the past,' it was said, 'as a part and consequence of the then current view of Scripture [as inerrant], emphasis was often laid on detailed prediction of facts, especially as concerns the life of Christ. We cannot now regard as a principal purpose or evidence of Inspiration the giving of detailed information about the future; but we recognise, as a consequence and evidence of Inspiration, such an insight into the Divine Mind and Will, and therefore such a general apprehension of the course of events to be expected in a world ruled by God, as in particular cases resulted in the prediction of events which subsequently came to pass. Nor do we rule out, as possibly a concomitant of Inspiration in certain cases, a direct prevision of detailed events, though it is not on such prevision that men should base their belief in the Inspiration of Scripture' (*op. cit.*, 2nd ed. 1950, p. 29). The Report implied a shift from the position that the fulfilment of prophecy made (inter alia) faith possible, to the position that faith might make possible belief in the fulfilment of prophecy. It could hardly be said, however, that on this subject the Report showed much awareness of the intellectual history of Christianity in the previous two hundred years.

The strength of Butler's position lay in his appeal to probability, to the steady building up of the possibility that Christianity might be true. In the nineteenth century he is the obvious master of John Henry Newman in a book like *The Grammar of Assent* (1870), which directly relates the idea of faith to the prior establishment of a high degree of probability, and of Mansel in *The Limits of Religious Knowledge Examined* (1858). The weakness

of Butler's position, on the other hand, was that he still relied on being able
to persuade his readers that there was at least a logical possibility that the
Old Testament prophecies were fulfilled by Christ and that the miraculous
events described in the New Testament actually took place. His method
suffered from the drawback that 'the mere logical possibility of an event in
no sense constitutes a *prima facie* case in its favour; it merely puts the
statement in a form in which we can ask whether there is anything in its
favour' (cf. the American theologian, Van A. Harvey, in *The Historian and
the Believer*, 1967, p. 86: this is an objection often ignored by twentieth-
century apologists whose attitude to the miracle narratives of the New
Testament recalls that of the eighteenth-century bishop).

Butler's consideration of miracles had in any event lost its force by the
middle of the eighteenth century. In 1748 the Scottish philosopher, David
Hume, argued that 'a miracle can never be proved so as to be the foundation
of a system of religion' (*An Enquiry concerning Human Understanding*, 1748,
ed. Selby-Bigge, 1902, p. 127). Hume defined a miracle as 'a violation of the
laws of nature' (p. 114), and made clear what he was referring to by the
example that he chose: 'It is a miracle that a dead man should come to life;
because that has never been observed in any age or country' (p. 115). Firm
and unaltered experience had established such laws, and therefore the
weight of the argument against a miracle – the Biblical reference needs no
elaboration – was as absolute as argument from the uniformity of experience
can possibly be. Hume said in effect that the narratives of miracles to be
found in the Bible could not be defended in general terms – the only way in
which Butler tried to defend them – but that each story must be defended
in particular. In dealing with the evidence adduced for it the historian
should not put aside his normal view of the natural order or his belief in the
uniformity of experience. If these criteria were rigorously applied the
evidence for a particular allegedly miraculous event would always be found
to fall short of proof, so that one was left at most with the possibility that
the event had taken place, but never with the certainty that it had actually
happened, and this meant that the miracle story did not offer a foundation
for a religious system. G. E. Lessing (1729–81) went further and said that
even if it were possible to prove the truth of the stories of Christ's resurrection, the contingent event in itself offered no proper basis for eternal truth.

Butler's *Analogy* offers one example of eighteenth-century theological
attempts to come to terms with the rationalist mood of the intellectual life
of the period. At first sight John Wesley's Methodist movement looks like
nothing more than a successful reassertion at the level of Christian behaviour
of the orthodox theological Protestant system (Wesley's understanding of
the doctrine of justification by faith, even his doubts about how to formulate
it, existed within the traditional limits of the reformed schools): the response
to his preachings belongs to the history of the Church rather than to the
history of theology. Or if one broadens the concept of theological history so
far as to include his preaching, it would be in order to note that there was
still, in the England of the eighteenth century, a section of the population
which, under the very guns of the Enlightenment, so to speak, clung to the
theological forms of the previous century and thought of the Christian life

in the terms of John Bunyan's *Grace Abounding*. The uniqueness of the Wesleyan response has been exaggerated, however: Lutheran Pietism, for instance, which, like Methodism, survived the eighteenth century, was a source, not a consequence, of the Methodist movement; French Protestantism also showed signs of a revivalist process in the first half of the eighteenth century; while the American revivalism which flourished between 1730 and 1760 (however divisive and destructive its final effects) had its own roots in the Colonial situation. No account of these national events which ignore what was happening elsewhere can be adequate, whether sociologically or theologically.

John Wesley's importance for the history of Christian doctrine lies elsewhere, in his doctrine of Christian Perfection, or Christian Holiness. The significance of his thought in this area becomes clear only if one places it within its European context. 'The period between 1648 and 1789', wrote E. Préclin (*Histoire de l'Eglise*, vol. xix, 1956, p. 519), 'broadly corresponds to the reigns of Louis XIV, Louis XV and Louis XVI. In that period developed the Cartesianism which in its turn provoked what has been called "the crisis of the European consciousness" and the anti-religious philosophical movement of the eighteenth century. At the same time, it is the period in which the political system of enlightened despotism installed itself and the bourgeois spirit formed. Secular attitudes became continually deeper and more powerful. It is not surprising that in this period conditions hardly favoured the foundation of new religious orders or new forms of the religious life.' In general, the dominant groups in eighteenth-century Europe rejected the traditional Christian model of the perfect life, the model of the man who had renounced marriage, money and freedom (including intellectual freedom), and for whom the highest form of sanctity remained in theory the absolute solitude of the hermit, an ideal which could be traced back to the Desert Fathers. This classical attitude had accepted the existence, on a lower spiritual plane, of the social Christian from whom less was demanded, who might marry, make money and act politically without incurring the wrath of God; but in the eighteenth century man in society began to deny the superiority of the ascetic, and even to deny his right to be an ascetic at all. Little serious contrast existed between the old ascetic model and the new secular one because little was tolerated: by the early eighteenth century the religious were widely despised and it is significant that in France, for example, the conventual life by no means cut off a woman altogether from participation in the society from which she had technically withdrawn. Professor J. McManners, in *French Ecclesiastical Society under the Ancien Régime* (1960), has powerfully illustrated the way in which the theology of poverty and withdrawal had ceased to function through the existing monastic institutions, which seemed both wealthy and interfering in a society no longer prepared to tolerate the contradiction between ideal and achievement for the sake of other, allegedly more spiritual benefits. One of the most convinced acts of the early French Revolution was the liberation – as its authors saw it – of monks and nuns from their vows; the secularization of conventual property in France was justified on the specific ground that the monasteries had no social contribution to make.

The Christian theology of holiness had always been torn between the needs and facts of a society at once hierarchical and wealth-producing on the one hand, and on the other the attractions of a theory of perfection which exalted the denial of one's self and the repudiation of anything which distracted one from the contemplation of God. Of course, sixteenth-century Protestantism had already abolished monasticism and the celibate priest-hood, had glorified the ideal of marriage and had also found ways of per-mitting divorce which implied that an earthly marriage could cease to be. But this was a kind of half-way to humanism, for the distrust of human nature which dominated the Reformed view of man made it necessary to believe that even if the life of the present world were not inferior to monasticism (or the priesthood) in the eyes of God, this was only because all forms of human behaviour were equally displeasing to God because of the corrupting effect of original sin. The Reformed tradition accepted the natural man but did not glorify him. The Protestant world remained psychologically subject to the older model of perfection for generations, as John Wesley's attitude showed, and as appeared in the very limited revival of monasticism in the Church of England in the 1840s. Although theo-logically able to repudiate the institutionalized forms of the ascetic theo-logical tradition, neither Luther nor Calvin could take a positive view of human existence. For them the model of the Christian life was the faithful steward of God's gifts and calling, one who no longer found it spiritually necessary to withdraw from everyday society because no greater conformity to the will of God could in the last resort be achieved outside than inside the normal human framework. This attitude flourished in a comparatively static society in which rapid and positive change was not expected.

John Wesley's originality for the historian of western religion and of Christian theology lies in his effort to devise a new model of the Christian life in an eighteenth-century culture which was rapidly divesting itself of the classical Christian assumptions about what constitutes human per-fection – the model of the anti-economic men, as it might be called. The ideal Wesleyan was to achieve a perfection as complete as that possible for the Desert Father, but he was also to live and work in the ordinary world without allowing his relation to God to be corrupted by his immersion in civil society: he would attain the goal of Christian Holiness within the pale of the Wesleyan Methodist society but without withdrawing from the world. Wesley was trying to recover the ancient goal of the ascetic while accepting, instead of resisting, the extent to which western society had already expanded economically; he wanted to place limits on the enjoyment of the social possibilities offered by society, but he did not want to limit the possibility of holiness. Theologically, he was not only reviving the idea of spiritual perfection in Protestant circles, but also seeking to preserve the power of religion as a limiting force on the acquisitiveness of man.

Wesley's doctrine of Christian Perfection may be examined in terms of two documents, a sermon called 'Christian Perfection', published in 1741, and an essay called 'Thoughts on Christian Perfection', issued in 1760. Both may conveniently be found in *John Wesley*, an anthology edited by A. C. Outler (1964), though the editor's insistence on the importance of Byzantine sources (especially Gregory of Nyssa strained through the writings of Macarius the Egyptian) for the proper understanding of Wesley's teaching on Perfection should be treated with great caution. Both essays have to be read against the background of the traditional view, common to both the Calvinist and the High Anglican systems, that perfection was a gift sometimes bestowed on the righteous on their death-beds, but usually only bestowed after death had taken place. Wesley's defiance of this tradition gave offence both to Anglicanism and to Dissent. In the 1741 sermon he quoted those who said that perfection would not be given in this world, but only at death, and he answered: 'How are we to reconcile this with the express words of St. John, "Herein is our love made perfect, that we may have boldness in the day of judgement; because, as He is, so are we *in this world*". The apostle here, beyond all contradiction, speaks of himself and other living Christians, of whom (as though he had foreseen this very evasion and set himself to overturn it from the foundation) he flatly affirms that not only at or after death, but *in this world*, they are as their master' (Outler, p. 270). In the same early sermon he was already trying to meet the objections of those to whom it seemed absurd to speak of any one as 'perfect': he did not mean, he said, that the 'perfect' Christian became exempt from ignorance or error, infirmities or temptations: he meant that the 'perfect' did not commit deliberate, conscious infractions of the known laws of God. They might suffer from evil thoughts and evil tempers, but these were internal difficulties to be distinguished from sinful actions. In general, however, Wesley did not argue from personal experience (this counts for much more in the 1760 document) but appealed to Biblical quotations to support his claim that '*a Christian is so far perfect as not to commit sin*' (Outler, p. 267).

These points were elaborated in 'Thoughts on Christian Perfection', dated October, 1759, but published in 1760. The early 1760s saw the climax of perfectionist teaching in British Methodism; a second, theologically trivial, wave of Methodist perfectionism followed in the United States in the mid-nineteenth century. Here again Wesley distinguished between sins properly so called, voluntary transgressions of a known law, and sins improperly so called, involuntary transgressions of the divine law, known or unknown. Someone filled with the love of God might still fall into these involuntary transgressions (which 'you may call sins if you please'), but was nevertheless delivered through faith from what Wesley seriously regarded as sin.

A change so fundamental was to be attained 'in a zealous keeping of all the commandments; in watchfulness and painfulness; in denying ourselves and taking up our cross daily; as well as in earnest prayer and fasting and a close attendance on all the ordinances of God . . . it is true we receive it by simple faith; but God does not, will not, give that faith unless we seek it with all diligence in the way which he hath ordained' (Outler, p. 294). Because of the difficulties which he was experiencing in London with antinomian perfectionists who believed that their faith lifted them above all normal moral regulations, Wesley was anxious to emphasize in this pamphlet that Christian perfection included moral achievement. This pamphlet, however, has also to be read alongside the equally characteristic

sermon on 'The Scriptural Way of Salvation', published in 1765, in which
he said: 'Do *you* believe we are sanctified by faith? Be true, then, to your
principle and look for this blessing just as you are, neither better nor worse;
as a poor sinner that has still nothing to pay, nothing to plead but "Christ
died". And if you look for it as you are, then expect if *now*' (Outler, p. 282).
This emphasis on the possibility of a sudden and complete transformation
of the personality explains the later use of the phrase 'instantaneous
perfection'.

Wesley compared this transformation, this entire renewal in the image
of God, with physical death, which might sometimes approach gradually
but nevertheless took place at a particular moment. He described, as an
event which he believed had happened to men he knew, a state in which
they could say, 'I feel no sin, but all love. I pray, rejoice, give thanks
without ceasing. And I have as clear an inward witness that I am fully
renewed as that I am justified' (Outler, p. 290). No doubt it was possible to
relapse from this condition, but the important thing for Wesley was that
Christian Perfection should be attainable at all. In the 1740s he had not
built the doctrine on the foundation of personal experience, but by 1760 he
was prepared to say: 'For many years I have preached, "there is a love of
God which casts out all sin". Convince me that this word has fallen to the
ground, that in twenty years none has attained this love, that there is no
living witness of it at this day, and I will preach it no more' (Outler, p. 298).
His alleged authority, that is, was the New Testament illuminated by personal experience; he emphasized the fulfilment in human religious experience
of the spiritual promises which he claimed to find in the New Testament. And
this was probably why Wesley told the members of the Methodist societies
that if they believed that they had died to sin they ought, on balance, to say
so publicly – advice which ran alarmingly counter to the apparent common
sense of the spiritual life and did not seem justified by its divisive results in
Methodist history. Nevertheless, this advice – that the 'perfect' should
testify to their perfection – played a prominent rôle in nineteenth-century
American and British evangelical history; in a more extreme form it was
taught that those who did not testify would lose the gift of perfection.
Wesley came close to this himself in 'Thoughts on Christian Perfection'
(cf. Outler, p. 289).

In the history of the Christian Church Wesley's perfectionism was a brief
episode. He combined the ideas of moral and ritual goodness – fulfilling the
divine ethical commandments and also sharing in the sacramental life of
the ecclesia – with something quite different, an experience of personal
deliverance from sin as such ('I feel no sin at all but love . . . have an inward
witness that I am fully renewed'). Moral and liturgical obedience could
be tested, but the state of grace which John Wesley described (without ever
claiming it for himself), a state which was supposed to be obtained as a
gift from God, given on account of faith and not works, could not be
delineated with any exactness, or effectively tested from the outside, so that
the pursuit of perfection was steadily discredited by some of those who
actually said that they had achieved it. Wesley, on the other hand, was
convinced that he had no right to disbelieve those who said that they had

been fully renewed, and constantly urged his followers to seek and expect this same experience.

Wesley's theological confusion is evident; his distinction between voluntary and involuntary transgression was too crude to bear the weight he attached to it; the stress on 'the conscious and deliberate intention of the agent is the most formidable defect in Wesley's doctrine of the ideal', wrote Newton Flew in *The Idea of Perfection in Christian Theology* (1934). One cannot safely define perfection as the absence of conscious sin. A more important weakness, however, was Wesley's willingness to describe not only the goal of perfection, but the way in which it was attainable. A man became perfected in a specific event, a conscious experience of God's gift of holiness. Wesley did not mean to depreciate moral and ecclesiastical obedience – indeed, he insisted on the value of the second far more than did a theologian like Soeren Kierkegaard, who shared his passion for absolute obedience to God but who felt that ecclesiastical obedience (a reliance upon the Church's understanding of what obedience to God should involve for a layman) positively hindered absolute conformity to the divine. Wesley's tendency to describe 'perfection' as a personal 'knowledge' that one had been freed from all sin by a direct act of God, however, led others to see the pursuit of holiness as distinct from the moral and ecclesiastical context, so that some nineteenth-century professional revivalists, for example, would 'offer' 'sanctification' in the same way as they offered 'justification by faith'.

The root of the theological problem seems to lie in Wesley's lifelong admiration for Christian mystical writers, especially Roman Catholic authors of the late seventeenth century. He accepted their utter devotion to God and their claims to a special sense of God's presence in their lives, but he rejected the Catholic theological framework in terms of which they explained their spiritual life. Instead, he tried to reach the same goal of 'pure love' by means of the Protestant idea of salvation by faith. He wanted to democratize the mystical experience, to replace the Catholic idea of process, of grace extending and perfecting nature in a handful of great saints, with a picture of God's grace as dramatic action, transforming the static misery of any sinner at any moment if only he begged the gift of holiness in utterly trusting humility. Wesley said that the gift of entire holiness was open to every faithful member of the Wesleyan societies. His theology of perfection, despite the weaknesses created by the stiff framework of orthodox theology into which he had to force it, represented an effort to keep the concept of God-centred behaviour alive in a society which was already beginning to find new bases for action in the market economy, the bourgeois ethic and the modern state. His approach was sounder than that of the nineteenth-century Anglo-Catholic revival of monasticism which pitted the old order of ascetic values against the new values of the expanding West without seriously debating whether the conventual life offered the most appropriate form of expression for Christianity in an urban, industrialized society dominated by potential plenty, not potential scarcity. The process of rejecting a Christian understanding of human behaviour and a Christian definition of the highest form of human happiness – a rejection already there in the Deist writers for whom Wesley's idea of 'perfection'

was a kind of insanity – reached its logical conclusion in Friedrich
Nietzsche's *Antichrist* (1895) in which Christianity was condemned fiercely
as a conspiracy 'against life itself', words which echoed powerfully through
European culture in the following seventy years.

Eighteenth-century Catholicism also faced the problem of reconciling the
traditional Christian model of the perfect life with the growth of the
bourgeois spirit. On the one side the Dominicans, represented especially by
Daniel Concina (1687–1756), whose *Theologia Christiana Dogmatico-Moralis*
appeared in 1749, thought that there was too strong a move to conciliate
the Christian life with the satisfactions of this world. They encouraged
confessors to press upon the laity moral demands which had in the past
been regarded as required only of those who aspired to the highest degree
of perfection. Benedict XIV, Pope from 1740 to 1758 (and thus a contemporary of John Wesley in his most flourishing period), supported this
reaction. Modern Catholic historians refer to Concina as 'half-Jansenist', by
which they mean that his moral austerity had much in common with the
mood of seventeenth-century Port-Royal.

This rigorism arose from a desperate anxiety to preserve the traditional
grip of the ascetic ideal upon the lay imagination: one may interpret John
Wesley's doctrine of holiness as a not dissimilar attempt to find a model of
perfection which could be followed successfully in the world of the Enlightenment. More like Wesley, however, was Alphonso de Liguori (1696–
1787), the greatest Catholic character of the eighteenth century, a man who
won the prestige necessary for his accommodation of holiness to the social
environment because he preserved in himself the ascetic image of the
persecuted saint who abandoned the world. Liguori's *Theologia Moralis*
(1752–55) slowly sapped the popularity of rigorism. It is impossible to
summarize here the subtleties of the controversy which raged between
'probabilists', 'probabiliorists' and 'equiprobabilists': what was at stake was
the degree of moral freedom which could be reconciled with Christian holiness in the laity. It is in Liguori and his order of Redemptorists (founded in
1732 as the Congregation du Saint Sauveur), and not in the medieval
Franciscans, that the significant Catholic parallel with John Wesley is to
be found. Liguori organized his order for the evangelization of the poor of
the remoter Italian countryside; he preached many missions himself, taking
as his favourite themes the fear of Hell and the safety of trust in the Virgin
Mary. Theologically, of course, there was a clear distinction between the
Catholic 'mission' tradition and Protestant Revivalism, which had roots in
the seventeenth century, chiefly in the American colonies, and which aimed
at the production in the individual of the outward and personal signs of
justification by faith, as a precondition to admission into the full membership of the typical local Baptist, Congregationalist, or Presbyterian Church.
Wesley and Liguori were not trying to do exactly the same thing, nor were
their methods closely similar, but both reacted to the spiritual and intellectual isolation of the lower ranks of an excessively rigid, hierarchical
society, and both wanted to awaken in people a greater awareness of the
importance of translating theology into human existence, especially where
the practice of holiness was concerned.

In its Protestant context, therefore, Wesley's doctrine of perfection represented an important attempt to revive the idea and pursuit of holiness (understood as a sinful condition, whatever the qualifications which Wesley sometimes applied), in a society which was now tempted to discard the idea of holiness altogether, and in which the Church, responding to the mood of the age, increasingly described the Christian life in limited moral terms. Wesley wanted to revive holiness as an absolute demand (as distinct from the instinctive relativism of the true moralist who knows – as Alphonso de Liguori knew, for example – how difficult moral choices really are), and yet at the same time leave a man free to fulfil his social rôle. To solve the contradictions which he created Wesley invoked grace on God's side and faith on man's side. His socio-economic dictum, 'get all you can, save all you can, give all you can', made peace with the new acquisitive market society which had broken with the scholastic economic theory. The scholastics had established the ethical basis of the just wage and the just price and had condemned unearned income in the form of interest. 'Get all you can' echoed the ethos of a society in which the self-centred pursuit of material gain was destroying the social character of property. This was not a revolution historically avoidable at that juncture, but a new theology of the Christian's life in the world was needed to cope with the results of the social changes involved. Give all you can, however, was not a solution to the problems created by capitalism; it only reflected the pre-industrial belief that individual charity was the appropriate Christian reaction to social problems. Wesley died before the full effects of the industrial revolution had shown themselves, but it was unfortunate that his search for a theology of intra-mundane holiness (the word 'asceticism' here only confused the issue, because it pointed back to the Desert and not forward to the factory) did not lead to a clearer understanding of the shape which society was taking and so to an earlier Christian self-consciousness about the full consequences of the expanding production of wealth.

The issue is important, because a theology of holiness can only really be assessed in practice. In the early nineteenth century Evangelical Tory parsons were among the pioneers of the Factory Movement, the agitation to reduce working hours and improve working conditions in cotton mills in northern England. The Evangelical attitude was summed up by George Stringer Bull (1799–1864), who said that people must have time 'to reflect, to improve their minds, to instruct their families and worship their God' (quoted in *The Factory Movement* (1962), by J. T. Ward, p. 423). The Evangelicals believed that the factories were forming a generation which could have no knowledge of the Gospel and must therefore inevitably be damned; the Evangelicals were freer to act in terms of this analysis because they were not socially identified with the men who were driving industrialization forward. The Wesleyan Methodists, however, remained for the most part hostile to the movement for factory reform: this was partly because their social connections put them on the side of the mill-owners, but partly because Wesley's concentration on the subjective evidence for personal holiness, his confusion of absolute obedience to God with states of emotional experience, blunted the practical edge of his teaching. By the end of the nineteenth century the position of the two groups had reversed: the Wesleyans supported the Social Gospel, which contained a very mild programme for moral, rather than social, reform; that is, they concentrated on symptoms of social disorder rather than on offering a new structure for society; the Evangelical Anglicans now saw any sort of social Christianity as a dangerous substitute for the all important issue of conversion, and so kept aloof.

The significance of industrialization for the history of theology is obviously hard to decide. There is often a tendency to assume that eighteenth-century European, and especially British, society had a moral and religious unity within which moral and metaphysical questions could be raised in terms understood by the society as a whole, even if there were no final agreement about the answers suggested. The Industrial Revolution, including as it did among its consequences not only urbanization but also the formation of class divisions, is supposed to have destroyed this unity and to have accelerated the secularization of society. In the twentieth century 'there remains no framework within which the religious questions can be systematically asked. For different classes the loss of a religious framework proceeds in different ways at different rates and in different periods, but for all there are left at last only fragments of a vocabulary in which to ask or answer these questions' (*Secularisation and Moral Change*, 1967, A. MacIntyre, p. 30).

Such an analysis does not seem to correspond to the real history of theology in the eighteenth century. Eighteenth-century society was already sharply divided into worlds which had no basic understanding of one another. Part of the social explanation of the rise of Methodism, for example, was that substantial groups of people who felt themselves excluded from the mainstream of English life and culture reacted by emphasizing their withdrawn status and by setting up a new society of their own, of which Wesleyanism, as an institution and theology, was the religious expression. The withdrawal of the Wesleyan societies from the Church of England was neither an historical accident nor the result (as John Henry Newman thought) of the absence of a concerted, conciliatory episcopal policy, but followed from the social origins of Methodism itself; the Wesleyan doctrine of Christian Perfection fitted in here again, as it happened, as a theological way of creating a separate Methodist identity. Eighteenth-century Methodism was not as potentially anti-social as seventeenth-century Quakerism had been in the person of George Fox; but Methodism should not be seen exclusively through the eyes of John Wesley, the quasi-Anglican loyal to the Establishment, for some of his ablest eighteenth-century lay preachers expressed through their Wesleyanism a rejection of the status quo.

In the same way, it is clear from the intellectual history of the Enlightenment that throughout the eighteenth century Europe was intellectually divided. Paul Hazard has emphasized the active desire of the Deist writers to be rid of Christianity: 'What the historian of ideas must first put down to their account is the immense effort which they made to transform into a non-Christian Europe the Christian Europe which confronted them'

(*European Thought in the Eighteenth Century*, 1963, p. 110). The myth of cultural unity, on the other hand, was defended by the American scholar, Carl Becker, who saw the philosophes as seeking to demolish the Heavenly City of Augustine only in order to rebuild it with more up-to-date materials. Becker's view, however, that the Enlightenment was a secularization of Christian attitudes, has not found favour with other scholars. R. R. Palmer, in *Catholics and Unbelievers in Eighteenth Century France* (1961), and L. G. Crocker, in *Nature and Culture: Ethical Thought in the French Enlightenment* (1963), agreed that although the anti-Christian writers were firmly embedded in a Christian environment, they were nevertheless advocating a new faith, one which involved a new stress on the possibilities of science, on the growth of the State, as well as a denial of the doctrine of original sin and all its alleged consequences. Crocker said that the controversy between philosophe and Catholic was concerned with moral rather than religious issues. In any traditional form the moral standpoint of Christianity contradicted that of the Enlightenment, and this meant not only that European culture in the eighteenth century no longer had a common basis, but also that in future European culture would not be limited to the kind of intellectual and emotional support which Christianity could provide. In its traditional shape, in fact, Christianity would become one marginal source of criticism of a culture which was accepting new presuppositions.

These changes took place in an intellectual context, from which social and industrial consequences followed, rather than *vice versa*. Between 1700 and 1750, when the French state was still able to prevent the publication of anti-Christian literature, deist and atheist manuscripts circulated clandestinely. There is an excellent account of these writings in J. S. Spink's *French Free Thought from Gassendi to Voltaire* (1960); through them the influence of the British Deists gradually permeated first France, and then Germany. The inevitable explosion came in the 1750s. In 1751 the abbé Martin des Prades, who was known to be a collaborator of Diderot's in the *Encyclopaedia*, published *La Jérusalem Céleste*, an essay in which he cast doubt on the apologetic value of the healing narratives in the New Testament. Pope Benedict XIV condemned des Prades' essay, and the Parlement of Paris suppressed the first volume of the *Encyclopaedia* in 1752; this made clear that official Catholicism, obsessed with its internal struggle with Jansenism and apparently careless of the sceptical influence of the Cartesian philosophy which the Jesuits had introduced into the seminaries, had no intention of trying to adapt to the rapidly changing intellectual climate of Europe. The Jesuits also bitterly attacked Helvétius' *De L'Esprit* in 1758: Helvétius, then a Deist, wanted to establish a science of ethics on the basis of John Locke's sensationalist psychology; his was a utilitarian system to which the pleasure-pain principle was fundamental. The persecution which he encountered shocked Helvétius into moving from Deism to atheism, and in *De L'Homme*, published after his death in 1772, he argued on mechanistic lines that all men began life with the same potential and that education could therefore be used to create an egalitarian, instead of the existing hierarchical, society. He proposed the redistribution of landed property as a further means towards the formation of a more democratic state. Down to about 1750 men of various shades of belief thought that it might still be possible to stand in a positive relation to the Roman Church, but by 1760 even this idea of cultural unity had also disappeared.

The weakening in the social prestige and cultural centrality of orthodox Christianity, which was the most important theological event of the period, and which went on parallel to the slow disintegration of the Ancien Régime, depended far less upon the effects of the Industrial Revolution than upon the Church's theological failure successfully to counter-attack the intellectual and political revolution which was also developing throughout the eighteenth century. What might be called the Church's social theology weighed heavily here, for rationalists like Diderot, Helvétius and Voltaire were all the more bitterly anti-Christian because of the justificatory rôle of the Church in the existing social order, and because of its willingness to use legal and political means to prevent the free circulation of ideas. Diderot's shift from deism to atheism between 1746 and 1749 coincided with his growing discontent with the state of French society as he struggled to publish the first volume of the *Encyclopaedia* against the opposition of the state and ecclesiastical censors. His imprisonment in the fortress of Vincennes (a state prison which also housed Jansenists in the eighteenth century) left him a convinced opponent of any religious institutions and of the non-democratic organization of the State. Even Voltaire, at one time an admirer of enlightened despotism, showed sympathy towards Genevan democracy in his later life. The intellectual atmosphere which these men formed made it increasingly difficult for either Catholic or Protestant orthodoxy to survive. The criticism of classical dogma from outside the Churches showed signs of succeeding where older internal forms of questioning, such as Socinianism in the late sixteenth and early seventeenth centuries, had failed.

External criticism did not shift power from the hands of those who opposed change, though it contributed to the suppression of the Jesuits in France in 1763. The internal demand for reform was theologically linked with Jansenism, which steadily became more of an attitude than a party after the Papal condemnation of the movement in the Bull *Unigenitus* (1713). The chief Jansenist leader of the early eighteenth century, Pasquier Quesnel (1634–1719) advocated an extreme form of the ideas of Edmond Richer, whose *On ecclesiastical and political power* had been published as far back as 1611. Richer said that although the Church was a spiritual monarchy with Christ as its King, the government of the Church on earth should be in the hands of bishops and priests united in one order and taking the advice of local synods, instead of in the hands of monarchical bishops with the Pope acting as both the source and sum of their diocesan authority. Quesnel now extended the rôle of the laity, saying that only the whole Church had the power to declare a member excommunicate, for example, a position which orthodox Catholic commentators treated as meaning that the laity might claim the right not to be excommunicated without their own consent – a liberty which official circles considered would be fatal to all ecclesiastical authority. Yet another eighteenth-century French advocate of a fusion of the Jansenist and Richérist traditions was

Nicholas Travers (1674–1750), who frequently suffered official persecution, and who, in his *Legitimate Powers of the First and Second Orders of Clergy* (1744), said in effect that parish priests ought to be free from episcopal interference. These ideas grew in popularity as the gap widened between the aristocratic and often very wealthy French episcopate and the more and more poverty stricken parish clergy. The highest point of these attacks on the system came at the gatherings of the curés which preceded the meeting of the States General in Paris in 1789. Many of the curés wanted a national, presbyterian Church, almost all of them wanted a thorough democratization of the system.

These hopes of change were not fulfilled in the French Revolution; a powerful reaction followed revolutionary attempts first to reform the Catholic Church and then to set up a new, deistic religious system in its place. In the meantime it was German, rather than French or British, theologians who tried to cope with the changing ethos of western culture. The ablest of these were Immanuel Kant (1724–1804) and J. A. Semler (1725–91). Kant summarized, in *Religion within the Limits of Reason Alone* (1793), a form of Christianity which might survive the criticism of contemporary rationalism; Semler, on the other hand, wanted to reform the presentation of Christianity from within the Christian community, applying to the Lutheran tradition in which he had been raised both historical and rationalist criticism. The difference that matters here is perhaps Semler's greater historical sense.

Kant began from the assumption that God existed as the moral ruler of the universe. This God did not require either the possession of conscious religious experience (in the sense of pietism, for example), or the deliberate performance of liturgical actions (orthodoxy) as a condition of obtaining his favour. Indeed, Kant laid it down as a principle which needed no proof, that 'whatever, over and above good life-conduct, man fancies that he can do to become well-pleasing to God, is mere religious illusion and pseudo-service of God'; steadfast diligence in morally good life-conduct was all that God wanted from his subjects. It was characteristic of Kant's position that he argued that the Lord's Prayer expressed the spirit of prayer so well as to make its own verbal repetition a contradiction; prayer was an attitude, not an incantation. If men really needed supernatural assistance in order to serve God, then God would provide it; the man who was striving for complete obedience to the moral law could trust God to assist him even if he personally remained quite unconscious of the divine presence.

Kant did not deny that man's nature was radically evil, in as much as he was a being capable of subordinating the moral law, of which he could not plead ignorance, to his own self-loving inclinations. Nor could the solitary individual overcome this radical evil in himself, and therefore it would be natural for him to join others in the formation of an ethical commonwealth, which Kant said might be called 'a people of God' because its purpose was to impress the laws of virtue upon the whole human race. The power of human evil, however, prevented the actualization of this community of virtue, and so Kant, ironically perhaps, called it 'the invisible Church'. The visible religious institutions of mankind were historical examples of man's desire to bring the ideal down to earth. They had anthropological, not supernatural, significance.

Kant linked this austere system to Christianity by arguing that true Christianity (which was not, of course, the Christianity available in the eighteenth century) came closest to the ideal. Christianity was the religion of Jesus and had no vital connection with Judaism (here Semler agreed). Jesus showed his understanding of natural religion when he said that religious practices such as forms of confession and weekly worship were religiously irrelevant, but that moral faith, which alone made a man holy as his Father in heaven was holy, was the only saving faith. Jesus' death was an act of perfect obedience to God, but the narratives of his resurrection and ascension had no value for rational religion; indeed, the concept of resurrection to be found in the New Testament writings was incompatible with any valid hypothesis of the spirituality of rational world-beings. When Jesus said that he would be with his followers to the end of the world he was thinking of the survival of the memory of his own teaching, example and merit. At every step in the interpretation of the New Testament the miraculous and the metaphysical must be subordinated to the moral. Jesus did not found the true religion because this had always existed, devoid of dogma (by which Kant meant especially doctrines such as the doctrine of the Atonement), engraved on the hearts of men. Jesus was instead the founder of the first true Church.

Even so, in the concluding section of the book Kant reduced the value of this best of all possible Churches almost to nothing. He disbelieved in the content of what was usually alleged to be religious experience and insisted that men could know nothing at all about supernatural aid. This made him regard the setting up of religious institutions as hazardous because religious rites, rituals and ceremonies constantly tempted men to believe that they were the witnesses of miraculous events within themselves. Kant, that is, did not believe that men should attach any importance to self-conscious religious experience. It was difficult for a man to be religious by himself, but once he associated with others in a visible 'Church' he was still more liable to fall into fanaticism and superstition. The Church's justification was that it stood as a sign of man's radically evil nature, but even this self-understanding men did not owe to the Church as a bearer of divine revelation; men could understand themselves well enough if they used their reason. The Church did not possess supernatural 'means of grace' in the sense that John Wesley, for example, would have interpreted the term.

The continuity between the attitudes of Kant and Locke is obvious. In the *Essay on the Human Understanding* Locke had already suggested that religious experience, which he called 'enthusiasm', held no significance for the truth of Christianity. Kant denied even more explicitly that there was an identifiably authentic, or validly self-authenticating religious knowledge of God available to men. He had no contact with such movements as eighteenth-century Wesleyanism, for instance, but it is not likely that he would have been impressed by the individual Methodist's claim that he had consciously received a divine gift of holiness. For Locke (in *The Reasonable-*

ness of Christianity), the religious significance of Jesus lay in his divine authority, so that when men accepted his claim to be the Messiah they also accepted his claim to show them the true form of religion, which Locke described in ethical terms much as Kant did. Kant, however, reduced Jesus to the founder of the 'true Church', since true religion needed no special divine revelation. The chief Deist positions seemed to both of them to be immemorial and immutable. They did not think of man's nature as a problem for which some kind of a metaphysical explanation was necessary; they therefore dismissed the classical Christian dogmatic system of divine special creation, fall (the doctrine of original sin), and redemption through the crucifixion of Christ, as well as the elaborate descriptions of the person of Christ (the Chalcedonian statement, for example) which this system required; they shared a rejection of the traditional concept of eternal punishment.

Kant did not bulk largely in the consciousness of most nineteenth-century professional theologians. They could do nothing with a man who sincerely thought that one would not go to church if one valued one's relation to God. In Germany, the influence of the Enlightenment on religion diminished during the national uprising against Napoleon; the Biblical critics, who traced their origin to Richard Simon and Semler, not to Kant, found themselves opposed by a revival of Evangelical conservative Biblicism generalled by E. W. Hengstenberg (1802–69). By the 1830s Hegelianism, especially as manipulated by D. F. Strauss (1808–74) seemed a more dangerous philosophical approach to theology; then in England Charles Darwin transformed the theological question of man into a historical question, and began to undermine Victorian self-confidence about the absoluteness of moral values. Ritschl (1822–89) is sometimes thought of in Kantian terms, and it is true that he rejected metaphysical speculation as a source of knowledge about God, but there was little that was Kantian in his return to religious experience, and to the Gospels naively accepted as the authentic record of the mind of Jesus, as data for a new, pragmatic exploration of the religious nature of man. Indeed, there was positive intellectual failure in Ritschl's assumption that only western religious experience was of any significance for his task, and that even in the west one should ignore mystical, pietist and Roman Catholic sources.

Kant's influence, sometimes undoubtedly at second-hand, can perhaps be detected in characteristic asides like Benjamin Jowett's dismissal of the Church as 'a figment of theologians'; or in Matthew Arnold's by now too often quoted assertion that men could not do without Christianity (like Ritschl, of course, he was thinking of Europeans), but that they could not do with Christianity as it was. Kant seemed to subordinate something he called 'religion' to something else which he called 'morality', whereas one hope of the nineteenth century – really in reaction against the Enlightenment – was to find a way of understanding religious experience which would justify not only the inherited western moral code (which had its roots in Classical Greece as much as in Christianized Judaism), but also speculative theology. Unfortunately, after Schleiermacher the task seemed to be too much for those who attempted it. There is no danger, in any case, of producing a Whig interpretation of theological history at this point; nineteenth-century liberals were writing on the retreat, disputing every inch of the ground but not contesting the verdict of history.

The Victorian liberal – Matthew Arnold for example – did not believe that the preservation of a religious interpretation of experience and the use of reason to examine the foundations of Christianity were mutually exclusive, but if he had to choose between the free use of reason and the survival of traditional religious positions he felt obliged to put reason before religion, as Arnold himself did when he argued that western religious culture had simply abandoned the concept of miracle in any common-sense meaning of the term. This acceptance of the autonomy of reason (rather than its omnicompetence) really entered the theological field in the second half of the eighteenth century; Christian Wolff (1679–1754), of Halle, for example, did not go so far; it was Semler's work that was fundamental to the change.

Kant and Reimarus had both seen the problem of Christianity from the outside; Semler was much more of a Lutheran, but a Lutheran in whom the historical, as well as the existential approach was deeply rooted. He was not prepared to abandon the idea of some kind of special biblical revelation altogether, but he restricted its use and importance drastically by a destructive (but to many of his contemporaries, liberating) historical analysis of the orthodox Lutheran theories about (a) the Canon of Holy Scripture, and (b) the Verbal Inspiration of the biblical text.

Semler historicized the Canon which, he said, was only accepted as such in the fifth century A.D. (Cf. his *Abhandlung von freier Untersuchung des Kanons*, 1771–75). This historicization was perhaps even more significant in its way than the late twentieth-century Roman Catholic historicization of the Tridentine documents. Semler argued that the Early Church spread through preaching, while collections of documents differed in different areas. A Christian could therefore be in the same position as Stephen, who had not read a line of what was to be the New Testament but who knew enough of the Christian faith to become a martyr. Only from the beginning of the fifth century A.D. did one find any striving for a single, agreed Canon. The institution had followed the Gospel, imposing a legal definition of membership, a creed and a standard documentary authority: in other words, the formation of the Canon was a practical and ecclesiastical act, which had no absolute authority. (Once again one encounters the disagreement between those for whom the ecclesia is in essence a supranatural body, and those for whom the ecclesia remains in essence a human institution). Semler said that if the formation of an agreed Canon was not essential to the initial spread of Christianity the existing Canon could not be made into a law for Christian faith and thought. He went further, because he held that for Christians only the New Testament message had a normative character, since Christ was the only ground of Christian faith: his dismissal of the Old Testament to an inferior status was again a portent for the future.

This demotion of the Canon meant, in effect, that one could not assume that every phrase in each book of the New Testament must have some profound religious significance because it occurred within a supranaturally inspired text. On the idea of Verbal Inspiration Semley was only a little less sweeping. He traced the notion back to the legend of the seventy translators of the Septuagint, who were all led by the Holy Spirit to use exactly the same words; while this fable was believed, it was natural that something like it should be extended to the New Testament. There was no evidence of a verbal inspiration theory in the New Testament itself, however; John and Paul, for example, appealed to quite other sources of authority for their statements, their acquaintance with Jesus or with the tradition which came from him. Semler thought that the development of the verbal inspiration theory could be attributed to an institutional need to guarantee the contents of the Bible, an attitude which caused his critics to accuse him of scepticism, and to see themselves as defenders of the whole Bible. According to orthodox Lutheran theory, the Scriptures might have been written down by men, but they were not men's words, but God's Word; it had even been claimed that the Holy Spirit dictated every word through passive human instruments.

At this point Semler parted company with the purely rationalist approach to biblical problems. He made a distinction between religion and theology. By 'religion' he meant an inner experience, a practical knowledge of the truth of God which was 'revealed' – he did not want to drop the word altogether – in the Bible. This 'revelation', however, was not to be lightly identified with the external words of the Bible. He substituted for the orthodox thesis that Holy Scripture *is* the Word of God, the view that the Holy Scripture *contains* the Word of God; and held that in working out the content of this revelation one should stick firmly to the historical method, trying to understand the text as the original author understood it, and not coaxing a mystical sense out of every text in the Pietist manner.

For Semler theology had become the scientific study of religious documents, a definition which he opposed to the orthodox Lutheran understanding of theology as a 'science of faith', and against the claim that the orthodox theological system, itself extracted as articles from the allegedly verbally inspired text of Scripture, ought to be binding on the faith of the individual. Semler, that is, like many later Lutheran theologians from Schleiermacher to Rudolf Bultmann, did not reject the essence of the Lutheran position, its concentration on the idea of personal justification through faith in Christ. He was prepared to affirm this in terms of his own inner religious experience, but he thought, as Bultmann was to think in a different intellectual context, that Lutheran orthodoxy had no intellectual right to make this inner reality a ground for requiring verbal adhesion to detailed confessional statements, to which, indeed, the historical method should also be applied. It was not surprising that he should have attacked Lessing's publication of Reimarus in his *Answer to the Fragments of an Unknown* (1779), though German scholars have sometimes seen this as a betrayal of Semler's own liberal principles. This was how Lessing took the book, for it cost Semler Lessing's friendship, but Lessing had in any case reached the view that the Bible was superfluous to the survival of Christianity, and found narratives like those of the Resurrection little more than an embarrassment in which there was no religious value. Semler, on the other hand, believed that the New Testament should remain a constitutive part of the Christian religion, a norm against which to test the empirical and existential approach; he had no sympathy with the Deist impulse (so strong in Reimarus) to clear the ground of Christianity in order to reveal the obscured simplicities of natural religion. One advantage of his so-called 'accommodation-theory', which proposed that Jesus was not completely committed to the Jewish thought-forms which dominated his sayings, was that it should enable the liberal theologian to separate a New Testament message from an Old Testament context, a context which Reimarus and many others had exploited against Christianity. (It may be added here that Karl Barth's influential account of Semler – in his *Protestant Thought in the Nineteenth Century* (1952, E.T. 1972) – which included him among the advocates of 'natural religion', was seriously misleading.)

In Semler many of the principal themes of nineteenth-century critical theology stand out already: the historical approach; the concomitant rejection of Verbal Inspiration theories; anti-dogmatism; the tendency to prefer existentially defined 'religion' to creeds, confessional statements and propositional theology in general. In 1800, however, such ideas had made little headway in the Christian community as a whole.

II

THE NINETEENTH CENTURY

The most important aspect of the history of nineteenth-century theology was the struggle for domination between two closely related theological outlooks or systems, orthodoxy, and what must still, for want of a better word, be called liberalism. On the whole, the initiative lay with the liberals in Protestantism and with the orthodox in Roman Catholicism.

In Protestantism the liberals sought to obtain general acceptance of the eighteenth century historical critical method of analysing the Bible. They tried to relax the binding-force on priests and laity of the historic creeds, denominational confessions, and other statements of doctrine like the Anglican Thirty-Nine Articles; they wanted to diminish the power and freedom of religious institutions to exclude laymen or ministers from the visible church on doctrinal grounds. Many liberals criticized orthodoxy as such, especially the traditional forms of such doctrines as the Trinity (see Schleiermacher's criticisms in *Christian Faith*, sections 170–172); the Person of Christ (see Matthew Arnold, *Literature and Dogma*, chapters 8 and 9); and the doctrine of the Atonement (see B. Jowett, 'On Atonement and Satisfaction', in his commentary on the Epistle to the Romans). The liberals promoted a non-dogmatic, and sometimes even anti-dogmatic approach to religious belief. They accepted willingly the advances of nineteenth-century science, which the orthodox were sometimes anxious to reject, but the direct effect of scientific thinking on liberal theology has been exaggerated by writers who have ignored liberalism's deep roots in eighteenth-century philosophy and historical method. Liberal theologians were not for the most part liberal because of the repercussions of a conflict between science and religion, or *Genesis* and geology; they were liberals because they already accepted the principle of free inquiry, which separated them from those theologians who advocated the absolute claims made for the religious authority of the Bible, Tradition, the Creeds, the Church or the Papacy.

Liberals did not accept, that is, the idea of a system of christian doctrine as a *revelatio revelata*, a definite message from God to man distinctly conveyed by his chosen instruments (the language is Newman's) to be acknowledged on the grounds of its being divine, not as true on intrinsic grounds, or as probably or partially true, but as absolutely certain knowledge guaranteed by the interposition of a power greater than human teaching or human argument. It was the finality of this conclusion, and the willingness of ecclesiastical authority, Protestant as well as Roman Catholic, to enforce it, which dismayed the liberal mind.

Schleiermacher, for example, did not dispute the use of the word 'revelation' to stand for a divine casual activity, but he did not think that revelation operated on man as a cognitive being, because that would make revelation essentially *doctrine*; instead, revelation was to be thought of as the appearance of a thinking being who worked upon the self-consciousness of those into whose circle he entered by his total impression upon them: doctrine was implied, but what was revealed and revealing was not doctrine in itself (*Christian Faith*, section 10). He then widened the idea, suggesting how difficult it was to draw any clear dividing line between what was revealed and what came to light through inspiration in a natural way. Moreover, if a religious body wanted to establish the validity of its own claim to revelation as against the claims of others, it could not do so by asserting that its own divine communication was pure and entire truth, while that of others contained falsehood. For if God revealed himself in this total way the finite human mind would be unable to grasp or use what was given to it. On the other hand, Schleiermacher added, an awareness of God which developed in a barbarous, degraded society might still be a revelation, even though it was grasped imperfectly in the mind in which it arose.

Here, cautiously, for he did not mean his words to be given too wide an application, Schleiermacher was arguing that if one started from the position that any kind of communicating relationship was possible between man and God, one was logically obliged to admit the possibility that 'revelation' took place outside as well as inside Christianity, whose claims to a unique and absolutely certain knowledge were correspondingly limited. Throughout the century the view that Christianity was one of a family of religions was to grow steadily in popularity; it was powerfully advocated by Ernst Troeltsch at the beginning of the twentieth century; the more exclusive view reappeared in the 1930s, but the liberal attitude returned strongly in the 1970s.

One has also to recognize the impact on the formation of the liberal tradition not so much of biblical criticism in the more technical sense – the historical effect of this has always been exaggerated – but of a freer kind of speculation about the historical career of Jesus, and about the reasons for the historical expansion of Christianity after the death of Jesus. The miraculous growth of Christianity, to take the second first, had been a fundamental part of traditional apologetics; as late as 1870 one finds Newman still defending the idea against Gibbon's purely historical interpretation:

> It was the thought of Christ, not a corporate body or a doctrine, which inspired that zeal which the historian so poorly comprehended . . . Now all this will be called cloudy, mystical, unintelligible; that is, in other words, miraculous. I think it is so. How, without the Hand of God, could a new idea, one and the same, enter at once into myriads of men, women and children of all ranks, especially the lower, and have power to wean them from their indulgences and sins, and nerve them against the most cruel tortures, and to last in vigour as a sustaining influence for seven or eight generations, till it founded an extended

polity, broke the obstinacy of the strongest and wisest government
which the world has ever seen, and forced its way from its first caves
and catacombs to the fulness of imperial power?[1]

By the 1870s, however, this was already rather old fashioned; the relative
position of Christianity in world-history was better understood, and it was
becoming clear that it was no more of a problem to give a purely historical
account of the rise of Christianity than it was to do the same for Buddhism
or Islam, religions whose supernatural origin was steadily denied by the
vast majority of western theologians. And the failure of christian missions,
at the height of European and American world-influence in the nineteenth
century to do more than establish marginal churches in China, India and
the Middle East – there was no question of replacing the local relgious
culture on any significant scale – reinforced the impression of late Victorian
liberalism that the world's 'great religions' were culturally bounded. In
Africa, Islam proved as lively as Christianity. And this slow change in the
psychological situation of Christianity reflected the changes in its historical
situation. For in Western Society in the nineteenth century the cultural
initiative largely passed to the secular minority. Quantitatively, religious
groups remained strong, but their rôle was never the same after the
American and French revolutions. A modern historian, E. J. Hobsbawm,
even claimed that 'in the ideologies of the American and French revolutions,
for the first time in European history, Christianity is irrelevant . . . The
ideology of the new working-class movements was secularist from the
start.'[2]

This was not the whole of the truth. The American revolution was
followed by a revival of Protestant evangelicalism which continued for
most of the nineteenth century; the language of this tradition was not as
irrelevant to the American Civil War as Hobsbawm implied. In France, it
was also an exaggeration to say that major political and social changes
were secularized: the revolution left France divided, but Roman Catholicism
proved strong enough not only to provide vital support to Louis Napoleon,
but also to endow the Vichy régime of the early 1940s with a social
philosophy. In general, however, his judgment stands, for neither the
American nor the French nor the later Marxist revolutions were based in
christian thinking, and a sense of the growing exclusion of Christianity from
western politics and much of western culture, steadily weakened, as far as
liberal theologians were concerned, any belief that a special providence had
watched over the rôle of the ecclesia within an otherwise 'fallen' society,
either in the first five centuries of the western Christian era or in the
nineteenth century itself. And of course a similar feeling of incipient
cultural superfluousness helped to stimulate the romantic conservatism of
theologians like Joseph de Maistre (1753–1821), the young Lamennais
(1782–1854), S. T. Coleridge (1772–1834), and F. D. Maurice (1805–72).

As has already been suggested, liberal theology was also deeply affected
by the so-called 'quest for the historical Jesus'. The most prominent

[1] J. H. Newman, *An Essay in Aid of a Grammar of Assent* (1870), pp. 458–59.
[2] E. J. Hobsbawm, *The Age of Revolution* (1962), p. 220.

contributors to the nineteenth-century succession of 'lives of Jesus' were
D. F. Strauss (1808–74), M. Arnold (1822–88), J. E. Renan (1823–92),
F. Nietzsche (1844–1900), Johannes Weiss (1863–1914), and A. Schweitzer
(1875–1965). The series of radically different images of Jesus which they
produced had really become logically inevitable once Reimarus (see above)
had shown that a coherent secular view of Jesus, in complete contradiction
to the portrait enshrined in the orthodox theological systems, was possible
in terms of the New Testament evidence. These new images of Jesus served
many purposes, including the orthodox 'lives' which contained a composite
biography designed to confirm belief in the traditional picture of Jesus as
the God-Man. All those mentioned here, however, were intended to help
men to free themselves either from Christianity altogether (as in Renan and
Nietzsche, for instance), or from Christian dogmatic systems which were
interpreted by the writers as crippling or corrupting western man – Strauss,
Arnold and Schweitzer all shared this theme. At the same time, the sheer
variety and subtlety of the 'lives' sapped the foundations of the liberal
assumption that New Testament scholarship, once freed from the restric-
tions of ecclesiastical censorship (which continued throughout the nineteenth century in the Roman Church), would arrive at 'agreed results',
and so at an agreed historical and theological understanding of the life of
Jesus. Orthodox theologians naturally welcomed the gradual diminution of
the prestige of New Testament scholarship; they thought that the discovery
that scholarship could not give final answers to the questions which it
raised would facilitate the reintroduction of a dogmatic reading of the New
Testament, and a reassertion of the Chalcedonian definition of the Person
of Christ. Liberal theologians, however, felt that what was happening was
the disappearance of the New Testament as 'scripture' (the kind of
document on which a religion bases its claim to absolute authority) and its
replacement by the New Testament as a literary document, not dissimilar
to the Homeric or Shakespearian writings. The distinction between the two
groups may be put in this way: that when the orthodox considered the
possibility that the New Testament was a book like any other, they rejected
it, whereas the liberals were not sure that the possibility could be rejected.
Behind this distinction lay another. The central argument of nineteenth-
century conservatism, accepted by all, Catholic and Protestant, may be
summed up in Newman's statement:

> Natural religion is based upon the sense of sin; it recognises the disease,
> but it cannot find, it does but look out for the remedy. That remedy,
> both for guilt and moral impotence, is found in the central doctrine
> of Revelation, the Mediation of Christ.[1]

In these terms Newman had spoken of the image of Jesus as the 'image of
Him who fulfils the one great need of human nature, the Healer of its
wounds, the Physician of the soul'.[2] Taking the nineteenth century as a
whole, the movement of liberal theology was away from that description of
human nature, and consequently from that picture of the function of Jesus.

[1] J. H. Newman, *The Grammar of Assent* (1870), p. 480.
[2] *ib.* p. 458.

Like Reimarus, Strauss, in his *Life of Jesus* (1835–6) tried to give a non-supernatural explanation of the origins of the Christian religion; but whereas Reimarus had cut Jesus down to a failed Jewish politician, Strauss interpreted him as a Jew who came to believe that he was the Messiah. Historically speaking, Jesus had probably been a Jewish religious teacher who had denounced sinners, foretold the Woes that would come at the End, and invoked the blessedness which would be the reward of the righteous. Popular Jewish feeling, soaked in a messianic literature, constantly pressed on him the rôle of behaving as though the supernatural intervention which he was prophesying had actually already begun. When Jesus died a community developed which, drawing heavily on the Old Testament, created a complete mythology, including the stories of Jesus's birth, childhood, miracles, transfiguration, predictions of the Passion, resurrection and ascension.

For Strauss, therefore, both Jesus and his successors were totally absorbed in a local primitive Jewish methology; it was legitimate, from Strauss' point of view, to say that if Jesus and the New Testament were to have any surviving significance, it would have to be in nineteenth-century terms, and in the closing sections of the book he used his own variety of Hegelianism to illustrate this. This was not a failure of interpretation, as is often said, but rather the assertion (which Strauss himself found it hard to hold on to in the 1830s but which came out strongly in his later work) that the New Testament mythology could only be given meaning if it was torn clean out of its historical matrix. If Jesus believed himself to have been the Messiah, he was essentially Jewish, and to take him seriously one would have to be a Jew; as for the ideas of incarnation and resurrection, for example, these could be restated in nineteenth-century terms, and this was the only way in which they could be given meaning:

> Humanity is the union of the two natures – God become man, the infinite manifesting itself in the finite, and the finite spirit remembering its infinitude; it is the child of the visible Mother and the invisible Father, Nature and Spirit . . . it is the sinless existence, for the course of its development is a blameless one, pollution cleaves to the individual only, and does not touch the race or its history. It is Humanity that dies, rises, and ascends to Heaven, for from the negation of its phenomenal life there ever proceeds a higher spiritual life; from the suppression of its mortality as a personal, national and terrestrial spirit arises its union with the infinite spirit of the heavens. By faith in this Christ, especially in his death and resurrection, man is justified before God: that is, by the kindling within him of the idea of Humanity, the individual man participates in the divinely human life of the species.[1]

After Strauss, the unity of the New Testament, and agreement between the historical Jesus and the primitive Christian community could never again be taken for granted; and in general liberal theologians were those who

[1] D. F. Strauss, *The Life of Jesus Critically Examined* (ET 1846), vol. 3, p. 438. There is a modern edition, P. C. Hodgson (1972).

reacted strongly to this uncertainty. There was, in any case, a considerable difference between saying that the New Testament contained historical evidence that Jesus consciously claimed to be the Messiah, or to be the divine Son of God, and saying that the primitive Christian community believed him to have been divine, etc.

On the conservative side, in the course of the nineteenth century, this was balanced by the view, already strongly held by Coleridge, for example, that the problems of the New Testament could be solved by turning from scholarship to religious experience. This was an appeal to experience to confirm tradition, whether Catholic or Protestant, rather than an appeal to theological tradition to interpret experience. One finds it in Coleridge's posthumously published *Confessions of an Inquiring Spirit* (ed. H. N. Coleridge 1840), where it was a step *behind* Kant not an advance from him, inasmuch as it was obvious that the experience was likely to confirm the documents when they were tested within the religious culture which they had formed. Moreover, in mid-nineteenth-century Europe there were fewer people really prepared to transpose their discontents into the language-game of the New Testament: anxiety and authority were shifting elsewhere. In 1843, for example, Karl Marx said, in his essay on *The Jewish Question*:

> We do not turn secular questions into theological questions. We turn theological questions into secular questions. History has been resolved into superstition long enough. We are now resolving superstition into history; the question of the relationship of political emancipation to religion becomes for us the question of the relation of political emancipation to *human* emancipation.[1]

This was a more seminal passage than anything in Coleridge, for Marx meant that the search for individual salvation, with which Coleridge was personally obsessed, was irrelevant at least until the social liberation of humanity was accomplished.

Although Marx, rather than Coleridge, wrote the agenda for the following century, the theological appeal to experience did not vanish. Thus the Roman Catholic theologian, Friedrich von Hügel (1852–1925), said not long before his death, and after a very close acquaintance with the personalities and ideas of the Catholic Modernist movement:

> But above all, and without any emphasis upon future possibilities, the essential, the most indispensable of the dimensions of religions is, not breadth, but depth, and above all, the insight into sanctity and the power to produce saints. Rome continues – of this I am very sure – to possess this supernatural depth – possess it in far greater degree than Protestantism, and still more than quite unattached moderns.[2]

This position – the verdict on Rome apart – might be shared by two distinct groups. The conservative proper could argue that if a particular

[1] K. Marx, *Early Writings*, trans. G. Benton; Penguin, in association with New Left Review, p. 217.
[2] L. F. Barmann, *Baron Friedrich von Hügel and the Modernist Crisis in England* (1972), p. 251; from a letter to Norman Kemp Smith, the philosopher, 31 Dec. 1921.

theological system produced sanctity there could not be much wrong with the attendant interpretation of the New Testament. A very moderate liberal like von Hügel, however, argued that if the orthodox theological systems produced saints, then their indefensible attitude to nineteenth-century biblical scholarship (and he had no real doubt that it was indefensible) might be endured. Of course, the use of the word 'sanctity' begged many questions, and it could be said that von Hügel had been educated into approval of a certain kind of person nurtured in a particular variety of the ascetic tradition; it was Simone Weil (1909–43), rather than von Hügel himself in his studies of Roman Catholic mysticism, who succeeded in making asceticism central to a twentieth-century religious outlook; but she had genius. The moves from religious experience to tradition and thence to the Bible raised another question, whether the spiritual patterns character-istic of the various theological systems could stand alone without the New Testament, which they were being used to interpret. This was the position which Renan and Matthew Arnold exploited in a liberal direction, the first without much respect for the Roman Catholicism which he had abandoned in 1845, the latter with more feeling for Anglicanism as he understood it.

It is sometimes said that the theological influence of Renan's *Life of Jesus* (1863) was negligible, that the book was only a stage in the discovery that there was insufficient material for a biography of Jesus which excluded the supernatural. This is an exaggeration, because it misses the sense in which Renan (and also Nietzsche) was concerned with theology as well as with biography. Renan used the biographical method to dramatize the difference, as he saw it, between the Jesus of the Gospels and the elaborate ecclesiastical and sacramental systems which claimed his authority. Jesus – Renan said – showed us for the first time the nature of pure worship, unbounded by either time or place, 'la religion absolue', in which the inhabitants of other planets could also believe. Here was the ultimate spiritualization of religion, with neither rites, priests, nor temples, a cult without a cultus, based on the Sermon on the Mount, in flat opposition to the actual historical develop-ment of all the major Christian churches, the Church of Rome included.

When Renan turned to the christological question, he said that it was permissible to call Jesus 'God', but not in the sense that he had totally absorbed the divine, or was somehow identical to it, but in the sense that Jesus was the individual who had enabled his species to make its biggest step towards the divine. With calculated vagueness, Renan implied that the universe had a spiritual core, and that Jesus had once and for all purified men's apprehension of how to find a personal relationship with this hidden source of being, 'l'âme cachée de l'univers'. No trinitarian doctrine was necessary, because the relationship between Jesus and the hidden source of all being was not different in kind from that which any man might now have with the ideal. Jesus had enabled men to take their biggest step towards the divine, but once the step had been demonstrated any one could imitate it who chose to do so. Much has been made of Renan's 'ambiguity', but he was not inevitably insincere when he said at the close of the famous preface to the thirteenth edition of the *Life of Jesus* (1867), that 'the least of the simple, provided that he worships from the heart, is more enlightened about the reality of things than the materialist who believes that he can explain everything in terms of chance and the finite'.[1]

It was said that Renan replaced legend with a novel: he certainly regarded the Gospels as legends, to be approached in the same way as European scholars approached islamic or buddhist documents. He said (in 1867) that if one limited one's account of the life of Jesus to what was historically certain, the result would be a few lines only:

> He existed. He came from Nazareth in Galilee. He preached attrac-
> tively and left in the memories of his disciples aphorisms which
> embedded themselves deeply. His two chief disciples were Cephas and
> John, the son of Zebedee. He excited the hatred of orthodox Jews,
> who managed to have him put to death by Pontius Pilate, then
> procurator of Judaea. He was crucified outside the gate of the city.
> Soon afterwards some believed that he was resurrected.[2]

Everything else was a matter of opinion, and the Gospels frequently furnished arguments for opposing theses. One could only suppose (this was the plot of Renan's novel) that somehow the ethical genius of the Sermon on the Mount was forced by the pressure of popular messianic expectation into a morally-ambiguous position, especially on the issue of miracles, from which death was the only escape. Death, however, liberated his pure conception of religion from the limitations of Palestinian Judaism.

Neither Reimarus nor Strauss had described a Jesus who was capable of founding a world-religion; in both cases the largely anonymous community had been the decisive factor. Renan's Jesus sounded like a religious genius, all the more so for coming into conflict with both Jewish orthodoxy and popular religious feeling; and Renan made him more plausible by the very act of historicizing him, by treating him, that is, not as the unique divine vehicle of revelation, but as a man who, over a quite brief period, saw deeply into the nature of the universe. And so Lessing's question about the gospel-stories, which had seemed so menacing – how could one base one's eternal happiness upon historical knowledge? – was at once answered and put aside. What mattered in the gospels was not, for example, the resurrection-narratives at which Lessing had jibbed, but the ethical understanding which could be tested in action. There was still a religious attitude here, Renan implied, and a valuable one, but it was simply not the religious system which the Christian churches claimed to have found in the gospels. Renan's way of interpreting the Jesus-figure appealed to the middle-classes in France, and to the working-classes in England.

The kind of distinction which was being made can be measured if one looks at Soren Kierkegaard's attempt, about twenty years earlier, and with Lessing's question specifically in mind, to decide what would be the minimum possible content of the Christian tradition. Kierkegaard's underlying anxiety was to make a case for the orthodox idea of salvation, an idea which seemed to Lessing to ask too much of one's reason:

[1] E. Renan, *Vie de Jésus* (Gallimard, Paris, 1974), p. 59.
[2] *ib.* pp. 44–45.

If the contemporary generation had left nothing behind them but these words: 'We have believed that in such and such a year the God appeared among us in the humble figure of a servant, that he lived and taught in our community, and finally died', it would be more than enough. The contemporary generation would have done all that was necessary; for this little advertisement, this *nota bene* on a page of universal history, would be sufficient to afford an occasion for a successor, and the most voluminous account can in all eternity do nothing more.[1]

Lessing had baulked at the traditional summary of Christianity because it required unconditional assent to allegedly historical events which could never in themselves achieve more than a high degree of probability, certainly not the absoluteness required before one could make them the basis of religious commitment. Renan's summary of the historically certain element in the life of Jesus, by its sheer brevity, delicately enforced Lessing's point, but left the possibility of an ethical theism based on the teaching of Jesus. Kierkegaard was prepared to grant that one could not base eternal happiness on historical knowledge (Lessing was right on his own terms), but argued that to stop there was to miss the point. The 'true' minimum historical account of Jesus was one which pointed back to the moment of God's self-revelation in the form of a servant as the first believers experienced it; this account was adequate to afford another man the occasion to encounter God's revelation – 'there is no disciple at second-hand, the first and the last are essentially on the same plane'.[2] At this point the statement that 'God appeared' was obviously a description of the belief of those who encountered Jesus in the flesh, the 'God in the humble figure of a servant'; as such, this belief was historical, and open to the historical method, there were even historical analogies. In Kierkegaard's mind, however, revelation did not consist in information which could be learned and passed on, nor was it simply given, to be taken or rejected, in the Bible: revelation was the self-authenticating act of God who revealed to a man his sinfulness and God's willingness to save him. Even if he had only the clues given in the short summary of the life of Jesus quoted above, a man could hope for the divine encounter, though its actually taking place would depend on God. What Kierkegaard had done was to surround human religious experience with the interpreting medium of a particular pietist tradition; the God who appeared in the humble figure of a servant had the rules laid down for him. Kierkegaard's attempt to show that Christian faith was independent of historical knowledge was to reappear in the twentieth-century theology of, for example, Barth, Bultmann and Tillich.

Kierkegaard, then, whose influence was to be felt after 1900, returned to the classical Protestant polarization of the repentant individual face to face with the God and Father of the Lord Jesus Christ, who in wrath yet remembered mercy. But mid-nineteenth-century Europe was not the world

---

[1] S. Kierkegaard, *Philosophical Fragments*, ed. D. Swenson, N. Thulstrup, H. V. Hong (Princeton University Press, New Jersey, 1967), pp. 130–31.
[2] *ib.* p. 131.

of the Reformation; the liberal, critical mood of the period may be
summed up in John Stuart Mill's view, in *On Liberty* (1859) that 'the
beliefs which we have most warrant for, have no safeguard to rest upon,
but a standing invitation to the whole world to prove them unfounded'. In
this atmosphere sensitive writers on religion like Matthew Arnold felt that
they had to abandon an apologetic based on the appeal to prophecy,
miracle, and the necessity of a divine mediator whose death was an atoning
sacrifice, and to work out instead a version of Christianity more closely
associated with the teaching and personality of the Jesus of the Gospels.
As he put it in *Literature and Dogma* (1873):

> The great prophecies of Isaiah and Jeremiah are, critics can easily see,
> not strictly *predictions* at all; and predictions which are meant as such,
> like those in the Book of Daniel, are an embarrassment to the Bible
> rather than a main element of it. The 'Zeit-Geist', and the mere spread
> of what is called *enlightenment*, superficial and barren as this often is,
> will inevitably before long make this conviction of criticism a popular
> opinion held far and wide. And then, what will be their case, who have
> been so long and sedulously taught to rely on supernatural predictions
> as a mainstay?[1]

As for miracles, 'our point is that the objections to miracles do, and more
and more will, without insistence, without attack, without controversy,
make their own force felt; and that the sanction of Christianity, if
Christianity is not to be lost along with its miracles, must be found
elsewhere'.[2]

Religion, therefore, had to be recast, and the first step towards that was
an understanding that the language of the gospels was fluid, passing and
literary, not rigid, fixed and scientific. The Bible, Arnold said, was not a
talisman to be taken and used literally, nor was any existing Church,
whatever its pretensions, a talisman for giving the absolute interpretation
of the Bible. Neither the historian, nor the New Testament scholar, nor
the traditional theologian, could save Christianity as it was. The cultured
layman who (as Arnold put it) had acquainted himself with the best that
had been known and said in the world, would have in the future to work
out his own interpretation of the Jesus of the gospels. If he followed
Arnold's personal interpretation he might, by means of the method (self-
analysis, repentance, self-renunciation) and the temper (sweet-reasonable-
ness) of Jesus find the joy and peace which came from the pursuit of
righteousness. For beyond Jesus existed an 'eternal power, not ourselves,
which makes for righteousness'. It is not clear how far Arnold thought that
one could observe the activity of this power in oneself. Certainly, he
regarded his description of God as verifiable; he substituted it for the
orthodox assumption, which he rejected on the ground that it was un-
verifiable that there was 'a Great Personal First Cause, the moral and

---

[1] M. Arnold, *Literature and Dogma* (1873), p. 152.
[2] *ib.* p. 189.

intelligent Governor of the universe,[1] from whom the Bible derived its authority; and he called the doctrine of the Trinity 'the fairy-tale of the three supernatural men'.[2] What he was trying to affirm was an ethical idealism which could still find in the Jesus of the gospels a principal source of personal moral power; to the extent that his position depended on Kant, he did not seem to see the force of the criticisms which could be made of the authority of the moral consciousness.

Arnold tried to compel Christianity to face the possibility of a purely human Jesus; he failed, and Anglican liberalism retreated into late Hegelian schemes for a Christ who would still be both human and divine; the same Hegelian pattern may be found in J. F. Bethune-Baker (1861–1951) and J. A. T. Robinson in the 1970s. Arnold failed, partly because he lacked Renan's ability to fashion a new Jesus-myth out of the old Jesus-myth; and partly because, once he had reduced Jesus to a Teacher of Righteousness, ethical imprecision set in. He has to be compared with Leo Tolstoy (1828–1910), for whom the teaching of Jesus (in whose divinity he also did not believe) was not just a matter of repentance, self-negation and (of all things) sweet reasonableness (as though Jesus had been a rather refined Oxford don), but meant non-resistance to evil, loving one's enemies, breaking up the traditional property-basis of western society, and so on. Arnold wanted to recast religion for the sake of stabilizing a threatened society; Tolstoy threatened society, and traditional western religion as well. One must not press this too much. Few Englishmen in the 1860s and 1870s grasped the quantity of human suffering which underlay national prosperity; in the Russia of the 1880s and 1890s Tolstoy was by no means the only intellectual who shuddered at the ignorance, poverty and oppression of the peasantry. Theologically, what mattered was that two such men should have agreed in turning to the ethical teaching of the Jesus of the gospels (however variously they understood it), and not to orthodox theologians who wove a supernatural concept of Christ into salvation-systems, Catholic and Protestant. 'If we now speak to a modern educated man', Tolstoy wrote in 1886, 'about the fall of the angel and of Adam, or about redemption, he will not attempt to argue or to prove the falsity of it, but will ask with perplexity: What angel? Why Adam? What redemption?'[3]

Orthodox theology had lost its grip on the culture, which in its turn was getting a grip on the gospels. The reassessment of Jesus was carried to a brilliant limit in Nietzsche's *The AntiChrist* (written in 1888, published in 1895), the most remarkable of the nineteenth-century studies of Jesus. Nietzsche dismissed New Testament criticism as irrelevant, because of the absence of adequate parallel non-Christian material from the primitive period. One could not arrive at what Jesus said, what he did, or how he really died, one could only try to reconstruct the psychological type of the redeemer.

Nietzsche interpreted Jesus as carrying to the furthest extreme a revolt against reality which he thought had become characteristic of the later

[1] *ib.* p. 12 (from the Preface of 1873).
[2] *ib.* p. 361.
[3] L. Tolstoy, *What Then Must We Do?* (1886, ET 1925), p. 236.

Jewish religious system. By flight from reality Nietzsche meant that
Judaism, already before Christianity, had used the categories of sin, guilt
and punishment to falsify the ideas of God and morality. God became a
God who made demands, in place of a God who assisted men; and morality,
instead of being an expression of the conditions under which a nation lived
and grew, became abstract, the antithesis of life – morality as a fundamental degradation of the imagination, an 'evil eye' for everything. The
offending and repenting Jew, as well as the wayward Jewish people,
constantly needed the priest and the sacrificial system in order to approach
God at all. Even Jewish history was rewritten, so that the great epoch of
the Jewish monarchy became a period of decay, and the Exile an endless
punishment for the sins of the great epoch. (Nietzsche would have noted
with interest that the Second Vatican Council was still struggling with the
question of the alleged responsibility of the Jewish people for the death of
Jesus.)

Jesus, Nietzsche argued, rebelled against the Judaism of his period, and
Nietzsche would have approved of this if he had believed that the rebellion
was directed towards a recovery of the natural values of existence, of the
instinct for life. Jesus, however, seemed to Nietzsche to want to retreat
even further from reality in the direction of a purely inner world. In his
interior kingdom Jesus stood outside

> all religion, all conception of divine worship, all history, all natural
> science, all experience of the world, all acquirements, all politics, all
> psychology, all art – his 'knowledge' is precisely the pure folly of the
> fact that anything of this kind exists. He has not so much as heard of
> culture, he does not need to fight against it – he does not deny it . . .
> The same applies to the state, to society and the entire civic order, to
> work, to war – he never had any reason to deny the 'world', he had
> no notion of the ecclesiastical concept 'world' . . . Denial is precisely
> what is totally impossible for him.[1]

In order to show Jesus in complete revolt against the Judaism he
experienced, Nietzsche had to assert that the ideas of sin, guilt, reward and
punishment were absent from the gospel which Jesus himself preached.
For Jesus every kind of distancing relationship between man and God (like
sin) was abolished – this was the essence of the 'glad tidings'. Blessedness
was not promised as something to come, or as tied to conditions, but was
the present reality. Jesus spoke only of the inmost thing: 'life' or 'truth' or
'light' was his expression for the inmost thing – everything else, the whole
of nature, and language itself 'possess for him merely the value of a sign,
a metaphor'.[2] A new mode of behaviour, not a new system of belief,
distinguished the Christian. Jesus no longer required formulas or rites for
communicating with God, not even prayer. He had settled his accounts
with the Jewish penance-and-reconciliation doctrine; he knew that it was
through the practice of one's life that one felt 'divine', 'blessed', 'a child of
God', not through penance and praying for forgiveness:

[1] F. Nietzsche, *The AntiChrist*, tr. R. J. Hollingdale, 1968, p. 145.
[2] *ib.* p. 144.

The profound instinct for how one would have to live in order to feel oneself in 'Heaven', to feel oneself 'eternal', while in every other condition one by no means feels oneself 'in Heaven': this alone is the psychological reality of redemption.[1]

Once Jesus died, Nietzsche said, his position was abandoned: 'the "Evangel" died on the Cross'.[2] Nothing could have been less like Jesus than the ecclesiastical crudity of describing God as a 'person', or of talking about a Kingdom of God which came 'upon earth'. Jesus had done away with the idea of 'guilt', had denied that there was a chasm between God and man, and had acted out of this unity of man and God as the heart of his 'glad tidings'; but the early Christians, inspired by Paul, unable to forgive or to understand Jesus's death, interpreted it as the sacrifice of an innocent man for the sins of the guilty. This was to construct the Church out of the antithesis of the gospel of Jesus. There had been no Christians at all in Jesus's sense, Nietzsche said; but instead a religion which feared and hated reality had taken his place, absorbed in an individualistic and superfluous doctrine of redemption. For Nietzsche, modern Christianity was the continuation of Judaism by other means. He denounced the orthodox Christian psychology of man, and said that in future men would have to find the courage to live without religious presuppositions, accepting their humanity, and neither asking their god to forgive them for it, nor hoping that their god would change it for them. Both the dogmatic, the ethical, and the simply historical images of Jesus had become irrelevant to the future of mankind.

The question of relevance was at the heart of the last significant nineteenth-century studies of the life of Jesus, those of J. Weiss, whose *Preaching of Jesus on the Kingdom of God* appeared in 1892, and of A. Schweitzer, whose essay, *The Secret of the Messiahship and the Passion*, A sketch of the Life of Jesus, came out in 1901. Both claimed that a 'true' life of Jesus must be based on a thorough-going eschatology, and allow for Jesus's apparent belief that the end of the age was imminent. When he summed up his views (with great éclat) in *The Quest of the Historical Jesus* (1906, E.T. 1910), Schweitzer argued that what he called the 'quest for the historical Jesus' had been an attempt to manufacture a 'modernised', 'relevant' Jesus, who would fit naturally into the feelings and aspirations of 'modern man' (whom Schweitzer himself did not like), whereas the 'true' historical Jesus had been a world-negating spirit, committed to the eschatology of his culture, and as alien to the nineteenth century as that century was alien to him. So far he resembled Nietzsche (whom he did not mention), but at this point he abandoned Nietzsche's line of advance and retreated into a liberal Protestant stance, for he said that although the historically knowable Jesus was irrelevant to the nineteenth century, there was also a Jesus spiritually arisen within men, to whom they could turn for religious leadership. Schweitzer's vague, ambiguous conclusion harked back to the positive side of Renan, but gave little purchase for further development.

[1] *ib.* p. 146.
[2] *ib.* p. 151.

If Renan's Jesus, ironically, was an eternal success, to whose simple spiritual religion all good men could return at any time, the typical Jesus-figure of the nineteenth century was a historical failure, whose teaching and example had been falsified by the ecclesiastical and theological systems which claimed him as a founder – a view which both reflected and influenced liberal ecclesiology. Renan and Nietzsche knew that no 'final' historical truth about Jesus could possibly be arrived at within the limits of the existing evidence; what they were challenging was the authority of orthodox theology, Catholic and Protestant, on the ground that neither could prove reliable links between the life and teaching of Jesus and their theological edifices. In the short term, this challenge hardly affected the history of theology, because there was an academic tendency to keep theories about the historical Jesus separate from 'dogmatic theology'. But the attempt to work from the Jesus of the Gospels towards a theology, instead of from a ready-made 'dogmatics' towards an image of Jesus, survived, and might be seen, for example, in later twentieth-century writers like Van Buren in the United States and D. Z. Phillips in Wales, who felt that the movement in modern philosophy associated with Wittgenstein had almost eroded the possibility of doing theology in the traditional manner, and who there-fore saw Jesus as the focus of a group of stories which might become part of the imaginative sustenance of man's spiritual life, but could not legitimately serve as the basis of a metaphysical system (see also *An Empiricist's View of the Nature of Religious Belief*, 1955, by R. B. Braithwaite, who underlined the links between his position and that of Matthew Arnold).

The conclusion of the nineteenth-century liberal movement, then, was a growing tendency to appeal from the authority of Scripture, Dogma or Church to an experience of the Spirit of Jesus risen, as Schweitzer said, among men. It became increasingly difficult for ecclesiastical authority to require allegiance to the language of the past, to the words of the Bible, the Creeds, the verbal statements of popes, bishops and Councils. Older views of authority had expected assent to the original description of scrip-tural events – the Ascension of Jesus, for example – quite as much as to the 'event' understood as symbol; now, not only the historical aspect of the 'event' was questioned, but also the value of 'spiritual', 'poetic' or 'mythic' interpretations of it. A Catholic Modernist like George Tyrrell, or a French Protestant like Auguste Sabatier (1839–1901), whose *Religions of Authority and the Religion of the Spirit* came out posthumously in 1903, held that the most that the official Church could do was ask for obedience to the Spirit of Jesus. This Spirit, however, was to be encountered primarily in the present, so that institutional authority as well as the creative theologian had to respond first to what was actually given in the present, instead of simply appealing to the record of a revelation given once and for all in the remote and perhaps inaccessible past. By the end of the century, in fact, the would-be transformers of the Christian tradition were no longer content with the idea that what was needed was to change the definition of the Gospel in order to bring it into line with 'modern thought'; they had ceased to believe in absolute theological definition or dogma; they were coming to believe that Christianity might have to learn how to survive without any ascertainable divine revelation at all.

This line of thought has to be traced back to Schleiermacher, who was one of a small group of Protestant theologians – the American, Horace Bushnell (1802–76), Kierkegaard and F. D. Maurice, for example – who were neither strictly liberal nor strictly orthodox (the word 'conservative' would often be more appropriate) and who, when they appealed to religious experience, did so on the assumption that experience would confirm what they still regarded as divine revelation, not provide a substitute.

Schleiermacher described Christian theology as the intellectual refinement of the Christian's redemption in Jesus Christ, a refinement related to the New Testament, but not unduly limited by its historically localized language. He took for granted that eighteenth-century criticism had weakened the authority of the New Testament, and that one should no longer use the Bible in the naive, non-historical fashion of seventeenth-century Lutheran dogmatists. (This recognition, however, had still not become finally established in the late twentieth century, and Karl Barth devoted his professional life to the assurance – rather than the proof – that Schleiermacher was wrong.) And he solved the problems raised by the Old Testament by arguing that 'we should entirely discard the Old Testament proofs for specifically Christian doctrines, preferring to put aside what chiefly rests on such support'. (Christian Faith, sect. 132.) The real meaning of the fact would be clearer, he said, if the Old Testament followed the New as an appendix, because the standard relative position of the two made it look as though one must first work one's way through the whole of the Old Testament if one was to approach the New by the right avenue. No more than his contemporaries was Schleiermacher able to cope theologically with the continuing existence of Judaism, but pressure to modify the orthodox Christian use of the Old Testament increased during the century.

In the opening sections of *The Christian Faith* Schleiermacher, over against Kant, argued for the trustworthiness of the subjective experience of absolute dependence which seemed to him the deepest element in human self-consciousness. It is generally agreed nowadays that 'a sense of being utterly dependent' is a better translation of *schlechtin abhängig*, the key phrase in the German, than the older version, 'a *feeling* of absolute dependence', because these words lead to Schleiermacher's being understood to refer to a shallow level of emotion quite distinct from the profound self-analysis to which he was directing attention. Nor was Schleiermacher adopting a pantheist position: he was saying that human self-consciousness included, and might even be summed up in, a sense of personal dependence on that which was outside and apart from the self, an experience which pointed overwhelmingly towards God. He made clear that he was not offering a proof of God's being (see *Christian Faith*, sec. 33). He defined the sense of utter dependence not as though it were an abstract proposition, but as an existential awareness that the whole of one's spontaneous activity came from a source outside oneself (see *Christian Faith*, sec. 4); this is best understood as Schleiermacher's paraphrase of the statement that in God we live and move and have our being. The consciousness of being absolutely dependent, he said, was the same thing as being in relation with God; on the other hand:

> any possibility of God being in any way *given* is entirely excluded, because anything that is outwardly given must be given as an object exposed to our counter-influence, however slight this may be. The transference of the idea of God to any perceptible object, unless one is all the time conscious that it is a piece of purely arbitrary symbolism, is always a corruption.[1]

Schleiermacher held that this primary relation with God was a universal element in human experience, and he explained the positive atheism of the eighteenth century by saying that while one source was no more than a sickness of the soul, a second and more important cause was 'a reasoned opposition to the current more or less inadequate representations of the religious consciousness. The atheism of the eighteenth century was for the most part a struggle against petrified, anthropomorphic representations of doctrine, a struggle provoked by the tyranny of the Church,' (*The Christian Faith*, sect. 33).

Christianity itself, however, could not have been worked out from this ultimate existential awareness of being in relation with God. 'There is only one source from which all Christian doctrine is derived, namely, the self-proclamation of Christ' (*The Christian Faith*, sect. 19). Christianity was distinguished from all other religions by the fact that in it everything was related to the redemption accomplished by Jesus of Nazareth (*Christian Faith*, sect. 11). In ordinary men the encounter between the divine and the human which was the underlying form of the human self-consciousness led only to unsatisfactory adumbrations of the relation between God and man. Jesus, however, had not just the normal human limited awareness of being in some kind of imperfect relation to God: in him the consciousness of God was so pure and entire that one might properly speak of God existing in him, something which could not be said of any other historical being. Of Jesus, Schleiermacher said, 'we posit the God-consciousness in his self-consciousness as continually and exclusively determining every moment, and consequently also the perfect indwelling of the Supreme Being as his peculiar being and inmost self' (*Christian Faith*, sect. 94). Christianity, therefore, did not develop from human self-understanding, or from purely human subjective aspiration after a possible god, but from God's prior act of existence in Jesus Christ, to which Christ himself bore witness in his proclamation of his relation to God.

Karl Barth, therefore, must be said to have been mistaken when he said, in his influential *Protestant Theology in the Nineteenth Century* (1952, E.T. 1972) that 'man, human self-awareness, determined namely as pious self-awareness, was undoubtedly the central subject of Schleiermacher's theological thought. In the very places where the theology of the Reformation

---

[1] F. Schleiermacher, *The Christian Faith*, ed. H. R. Mackintosh, p. 18, from 2nd German ed. 1830; 1st ed. 1821–22; I use this as the basis of Schleiermacher's mature view. See also R. B. Brandt, *The Philosophy of Schleiermacher* (Westport, Conn., U.S.A., 1941, repr. 1971).

had said "the Gospel" or "the Word of God" or "Christ" Schleiermacher, three hundred years after the Reformation, now says religion or piety . . . Schleiermacher reversed the order of this thought. What interests him is the question of man's action in regard to God.'[1] The idea of God acting creatively upon and within man through Christ was essential to Schleiermacher's system. Writing in 1917, Rudolf Bultmann, in many ways one of Schleiermacher's heirs, said that the Christian faith was a relationship of God to man 'which is achieved neither by rational considerations nor by natural necessities but by experiences which are given to man outside reason and nature, which overpower him, to which he surrenders himself freely, which he describes as revelation, grace; in which he knows that he is not independently creative, as in other areas of culture, but quite simply dependent'.[2] This theocentric emphasis was constantly present in Schleiermacher's dogmatics, and was characteristic of his christology, which was a courageous attempt to replace the static logical impossibilities of the chalcedonian Christ of the two natures with something more dynamic and more intelligible.

In Schleiermacher's account the existence of God in the Redeemer was posited as the fundamental power within him. Everything in him that was human simply constituted the organism for this fundamental and divine power, and was related to it in the same way as in ordinary people all other human powers were related to the controlling intelligence. Since the Redeemer's human activity depended entirely upon God's presence with him, it was reasonable, Schleiermacher argued, to say that in his case (and in his alone) God became man. His human life sprang out of the divine. (See *Christian Faith*, sect. 96, pp. 397–8).

Many German Protestant theologians followed Schleiermacher in his rejection of the Chalcedon settlement (see *Christian Faith*, sect. 95–97, pp. 389–413), including Ritschl and Troeltsch. His skill in moving between liberal necessities and conservative absolutes was also clear in his treatment of the doctrine of the Virgin Birth. To begin with, he said that the Redeemer could not have come into being through natural procreation, because he must not belong to the corporate life of human sinfulness. Moreover, 'the reproductive power of the species cannot be adequate to produce an individual through whom something is to be introduced for the first time into the species which was never in it before' (*Christian Faith*, sect. 97). To achieve the desired end one had to postulate, in addition to the reproductive power of the species, a creative activity combined with the human activity. 'In this sense anyone who assumes in the Redeemer a natural sinlessness' – and Schleiermacher argued that sinlessness was natural, not unnatural, to man – 'and a new creation through the union of the divine with the human, postulates a supernatural conception as well'. Nevertheless, the assumption of a virgin birth in the traditional sense was superfluous, because 'the being of God in life cannot be explained by its origin from a virgin without sexual intercourse'. Consequently, everything turned upon 'the higher influence which as a divine creative activity could alter

[1] K. Barth, *Protestant Theology in the Nineteenth Century* (ET 1972), pp. 458–59.
[2] W. Schmithals, *Introduction to Bultmann's* Theology (ET 1968), p. 8.

both the paternal and the maternal influence in such a way that all ground
for sinfulness was removed, and this although procreation was perfectly
natural . . . The general idea of a supernatural conception remains . . .
essential and necessary if the specific pre-eminence of the Redeemer is to
remain undiminished. But the more precise definition of this supernatural
conception as one in which there was no male activity has no connection of
any kind with the essential elements in the peculiar dignity of the Redeemer;
and hence, in and by itself, is no constituent part of Christian doctrine.'

Schleiermacher allowed that one might accept the traditional doctrine
on the ground of the narratives contained in the New Testament, but
anyone who could not accept these stories as literally and historically true
was still free to hold a doctrine of the supernatural conception constructed
along the lines which Schleiermacher suggested. In the same way, belief
in the traditional doctrines of Jesus's resurrection, descent into Hell,
ascension and return in judgment was not an independent element in the
original faith in Christ, of such a kind that one could not accept him as the
redeemer or recognize the being of God in him if one did not know that he
had risen from the dead and ascended into heaven and so forth: all that
was required from a Protestant, Schleiermacher said, was that he believe
in these stories as far as he thought they were adequately attested in the
New Testament – a conclusion which meant that these propositions
belonged to the area of biblical studies – where they would remain indefinitely – and not to the doctrine of the.Person of Christ at all (*Christian
Faith*, sect. 99).

Schleiermacher, that is, was discounting the impact of biblical criticism
before many Catholics or Protestants had begun to feel its full power. He
sought to persuade his contemporaries that they did not have to defend
the literal and historical sense of every New Testament story, as though the
truth or untruth of Christianity as a religion of redemption through Jesus
Christ depended upon the credibility, for instance, of the resurrection
stories as traditionally understood – a position as hazardous, though often
adopted in the mid-twentieth century, as that which committed the cause
of Victorian Christianity to the historical reliability of the Genesis creation-
stories. On the one hand, the basic element in 'religion' (the sense of utter
dependence) was a universal and necessary part of human experience; it
could exist without either the knowledge of, or assent to, doctrines as such,
because it was an immediate existential relation to God. On the other hand,
given that every human being had an innate capacity for being religious,
'Christianity' in particular was the result of the play of Jesus's perfect
religious consciousness on the developing religious consciousness of those
human beings who were brought within the field of influence of the Christian
tradition. From Schleiermacher's point of view, his systematic theology
was an empirical description of the experience of those who had been
redeemed by the activity of Christ and made members of a spiritual
community whose creative energy came from Christ. He could therefore
demonstrate inadequacies in both the New Testament and traditional
theological systems by comparing them with the empirical evidence of
experience. For him, the New Testament was simply the original but not

inherently final attempt to describe the nature of Christian redemption, while documents like the Creeds and the Confessions of the Reformation tradition (which he discussed at length in *The Christian Faith*)[1] were equally imperfect attempts to reduce piety to language, a process which frequently confused philosophical and religious method.

The value of Schleiermacher's enterprise depended, of course, on the question of the relationship between religion and philosophy. At times in *The Christian Faith* he seemed only to claim that theology was a description of the content and convictions of the religious consciousness, and did not raise the question of their truth. At other times, he seemed to assert that a religious person had a direct experience of the divine object, and that this made religion independent of philosophy. In the second instance, he has been criticized for not clearly facing the issue of the truth or falsity of the claim: to do so would have taken him back into philosophical territory.[2]

If one says that Schleiermacher was neither strictly liberal nor strictly orthodox, but perhaps 'conservative', it is because a candid reading of *The Christian Faith* leaves the impression that Schleiermacher was trying to restate in acceptable ethical and psychological terms as much as possible of the traditional doctrinal pattern, in which a more than human Christ redeemed the human race from sin and bound it together in a new company of perfect love: this was the barest possible summary of the Christian 'myth', without which a recognizable Christian tradition would have ceased to exist; that it was not easy to demonstrate the truth of the myth did not mean that it was no more than false. Thus he could write: 'Just as the redemptive activity of Christ brings about for all believers a corporate activity corresponding to the being of God in Christ, so the reconciling element, that is, the blessedness of the being of God in him, brings about for all believers, as for each separately, a corporate feeling of blessedness.' In this spiritual process their former personality, the 'old man' of traditional theology, died, to be replaced by a new kind of self-identity, which owed its whole existence to the creative activity of Christ. A 'new man' took the place of the old, a 'new man' who, nevertheless, somehow retained continuity with his individual past. There was no question of the redeemed losing their identity in a vague, corporate holiness; instead, they attained a new kind of individuality, perfectly related to one another in Christ (*Christian Faith*, sect. 101, p. 436).

Such an exposition was based entirely, Schleiermacher said, on the inner experience of the believer; it could make no claim to be proof of the absolute truth of what was stated; but unless something like this was the case there would be no special possession of divine grace in Christianity at all. This distinction between a moral consciousness (the chief ground of the liberal position) and a state of consciousness which was held to contain an immediate experience of God, linked Schleiermacher with conservatives like Coleridge, Maurice and Kierkegaard. His position was much closer to orthodoxy than the rather vague appeal to the Spirit of Jesus as a divine

---

[1] See e.g. Section 109, pp. 496–505, where Schleiermacher comments on the doctrine of justification.

[2] See R. B. Brandt, *op. cit.*, pp. 294–98.

agent of change, an Arnoldian moral leader with a programme as well as a method, which was to characterize late-nineteenth-century liberalism. Both, in turn, were menaced by the tightening, in Germany in particular, of the anti-supernatural screw, first by Ludwig Feuerbach (1804–72), the materialist philosopher, who said in *The Essence of Christianity* (1841, E.T. by George Eliot, 1854) that men made themselves unhappy by projecting as an idea of 'God' a dream of human perfection which they could never realize, and that so-called 'religious experiences', while real enough, were nevertheless no more than subjective: Feuerbach, however, like some twentieth-century Christian liberals, assumed that 'religious' behaviour was part of the essence of human nature, and would continue even when deprived of its supernatural object. Second, by Karl Marx (1818–83), in his *Critique of Hegel's Philosophy of Right* (1844) and the *Theses on Feuerbach* (1845), who said that the religious sentiment was not a matter of individual psychology, as Feuerbach thought, but a social product. Certainly, man made religion and not religion man, but he did so only because the conditions of a particular society in historical time alienated him from his potential self. Religion might be the sigh of the oppressed but it was also the opium of the people. To ask men to give up their religious comforts and illusions was to ask them to give up the social conditions which made the illusions necessary. Revolutionize the society and religions would disappear, because it would no longer be socially generated.

Although few orthodox theologians can have read Marx they were aware that the connection between the 'natural' and the 'supernatural' had somehow to be maintained, and it is significant that this was a period of intense christological ingenuity. G. Thomasius (1802–75) and W. R. Gess (1819–71), among others, proposed a kenotic ('self-divesting') christology, in which they implied that the Eternal Son suppressed as much of his divinity during his earthly life as was necessary to make the idea of the incarnation credible theologically in the nineteenth century. In Gess's version the suppression was actually total, so that throughout his Palestinian existence the Eternal Son was simply a man. This was a desperate, unorthodox orthodoxy, aware that a case had to be made for the divinity of Christ but driven to make it by emphasizing his humanity. Moreover, romantic moves to revive the great theological systems of the past in order to establish the roots of modern orthodoxy in heroic soil, such as one sees in Anglo-Catholicism and Anglican Evangelicalism, or in the German Reformed 'Mercersburg Theology' in the United States (1844–53), failed in so far as they were unable to restate the supernatural argument convincingly. In British terms the change of mood could be seen clearly in the bitterness with which H. P. Liddon (1829–90), a rigid Anglo-Catholic of Keble's school, who had produced in *The Divinity of Our Lord and Saviour Jesus Christ* (1867) a consciously naive, biblicist and patristic, orthodox christology, received as a betrayal the belated kenotic speculations of Charles Gore (1853–1932) in the collection of Anglo-Catholic essays, *Lux Mundi* (1889). It was obviously not an accident that Gore belonged to the generation of Anglo-Catholics who preached Christian Socialism and founded monastic orders, just as Ritschl, though anti-socialist politically, vaguely identified the Kingdom of God with a regenerated world-common-wealth and, in abandoning Chalcedon, substituted a moral appraisal of a traditionally visualized New Testament Jesus who was held to have the value of God for the mind of faith. A slow shift of interest was taking place from what had in the past been believed or felt about a supernatural Christ, to what could be allegedly recognized as evidence that God (or Christ) was at work in the world.

This shift of interest stranded – as far as fashion went – the great conservatives of the period, Kierkegaard and Newman; even Maurice owed his nineteenth-century influence to his social teaching (see p. 548). For Maurice, who combined a Platonic epistemology with biblical ideas of God as the personal will of love acting in and through Christ, was convinced that man could participate in the eternal world when the true knowledge of reality was given him by Christ.[1] This was why he reacted so violently against the Oxford philosopher of religion, H. L. Mansel (1820–71) when he said in *The Limits of Religious Thought Examined* (1859) that man's knowledge was conditioned by time and space and that therefore he could not conceive God as he truly is; neither a sense of dependence nor a sense of moral obligation contained a direct intuition of God, but that men were entirely dependent for real knowledge of God on an objective, divine self-revelation, by which Mansel meant the Bible. 'Religion, to be a relation between God and Man at all, must rest on a belief in the Infinite, and also on a belief in the Finite: if we deny the first, there is no God; and if we deny the second, there is no Man. But the co-existence of the Infinite and the Finite in any manner whatever is inconceivable by reason; and the only ground that can be taken for accepting one representation of it rather than another, is that one is revealed and the other is not revealed.'[2] Strictly speaking, Mansel regarded the Bible, Old as well as New Testament, as set apart from any kind of criticism, to be accepted or rejected as revelation; but since he held that speculative theology was only a product of man's limited reason, he thought of the Bible as containing what he called 'representative revelation', revelation, that is, by means of symbols drawn from human experience, anthropomorphic, and therefore inevitably less than a full revelation of the nature of God. Mansel's book was a sign of what was to come philosophically; indeed, it probably helps to explain why Matthew Arnold was so willing to criticize the freedom with which many Victorian theologians talked of their 'knowledge' of God.

For Maurice, however, as for Coleridge, it was axiomatic that all men possessed a faculty by which they could attain direct communion with God, provided they reached out toward him and let him impart it. In Kantian terms, Maurice simply asserted that God gave men the direct knowledge of himself which the Pure Reason could not obtain according to Kant, because it was limited to regulative or constitutive ideas which had only an empirical use and could not be extended to objects which transcended experience, like God. Maurice's efforts to defend his position rarely got

[1] T. B. Christensen, *The Divine Order, a Study in F. D. Maurice's Theology* (Leiden 1973), pp. 65–73.
[2] H. L. Mansel, *The Limits of Religious Thought Examined* (1859), p. 125.

further than a vague mysticism: 'There is a light within you, close to you
. . . Turn from these idols that are surrounding you – from the confused,
dark world of thoughts within you. It will reveal itself to you . . . I mean
a reality; I mean that which has to do with your innermost being; I mean
something which does not proceed from you or belong to you; but which is
there searching you and judging you . . . I mean that this light comes from
a Person . . . from the Word, the Son of God . . . Turn and confess his
presence. You have always had it with you.'[1]

At this point, at which the familiar Victorian attempt to personalize
conscience – it was the core, for example, of Newman's *Grammar of Assent*
(1870) – was transformed into the assertion that the Person of Christ was
always actively present in each individual, one is reminded of Schleiermacher's idea of salvation, and there were other similarities, in Maurice's
implicit universalism and vigorous rejection of penal substutionary theories
of the atonement. Both men had a profound belief in the existence of a
Divine Order (as opposed to disorder) which had to be revealed (not
restored). In the long run, however, it was Maurice's *social* exposition of his
principles which found disciples (see p. 533); it was only in the twentieth
century that A. M. Ramsey, for instance,[2] praised Maurice for holding the
'classic' conception of the Cross as the divine victory over the powers of
evil. The Danish authority on Maurice, T. B. Christensen (in 1973) criticized
this assertion on the ground that the 'classic' theory presupposed exactly
the kind of *disorder* in the universe which Maurice found theologically
incredible.[3] Maurice's brilliant combination of the Bible and Plato,
Christensen concluded, had not exercised any great influence on the
emergence and shaping of modern English theology. This was partly
because Maurice did not cope adequately with the problem of the authority
of the Bible, and partly because later theologians (von Hügel being the
obvious exception) did not find Platonism a solution to their difficulties
with contemporary philosophy. Much the same comment might be made
on Coleridge, whose influence in this field has been exaggerated, especially
by literary critics.

Although Soeren Kierkegaard was a greater writer and theologian than
Maurice, he was equally isolated in the nineteenth century. He started with
the handicap of writing in Danish, but even if he had been translated more
quickly he would probably still have been disregarded, for he not only
denied that the God of Danish Lutheranism had any significant relation to
the God of Luther, but he also rejected the Hegelian alternative of a God
identifiable with, and discoverable in, the historical process. Moreover, he
remained faithful to the eighteenth-century pietist tradition at the very
time – 1800 to 1848 – when Pietism in general, and German Pietism of the
Hengstenberg era in particular, was abandoning its old indifference to social
and political concerns and becoming the staunch ally of those who were
resisting political change, a development which reached a fateful climax in
1848 when most Protestant leaders opposed the liberal political revolutions.

[1] F. D. Maurice, *Theological Essays* (1853), pp. 117–18.
[2] See A. M. Ramsey, *F. D. Maurice and the Conflicts of Modern Theology* (1951).
[3] Christensen, esp. pp. 197–220.

Kierkegaard was nearer the heart of the Pietist tradition when he claimed that the demands of God, properly understood, could only destroy society in any normal form. It was not possible, he said, to love God in the Christian sense and to be happy in this world. With a very different emphasis from Maurice's, he said that the Christian God was in opposition to the fallen creation; indeed, Kierkegaard's late enthusiasm for celibacy was a way of expressing this position: Christianity was not only salvation from the human race, but it also aimed at stopping the human process.

For Kierkegaard was so far outside the contemporary approach to truth through history – to be found in Hegel, Marx, Spencer, and even Maurice when, as in *The Kingdom of Christ* (1838), he upheld both the nation and the British Established Church as divine institutions serving divine purposes – that he denied that Christianity had any history at all after the historical paradox of its origin, that the eternal came into existence *once* in time (see *Authority and Revelation*, E.T. Princeton 1955). Christendom, by which he meant the unity of state, religion and society which had been so familiar to Europe as to be accepted without question as of divine origin, might have had a history, but this was irrelevant, except in so far as it tempted men to rely on 'the faith of their fathers' for salvation, instead of facing the New Testament for themselves and Christ as their contemporary. For Kierkegaard, Christianity-as-Truth had been revealed once and for all, and historical time was dangerous, because the human apprehension of divine truth actually appeared to lessen as time went on: nineteenth-century Danish Lutheranism was further from the New Testament truth than Luther himself had been.

As for Hegel, his assertion that divine truth was not given once and for all, but unfolded itself gradually through the history of the race and the universe, inevitably involved a claim to judge the Christ-event itself, when it was by the Christ-event that men themselves were to be tested. In effect, by saying that absolute truth appeared only at the end of the historical process, Hegel relativized truth at any particular point of time, and Marx dramatized this when, in *The Communist Manifesto* (1848), he relativized the leading ideas of any epoch as being only the ideas of its ruling class. Both subsumed the individual in the general history of race and class, denying that he could experience any kind of eternal truth for himself.

Kierkegaard reversed this. The Christian category was the single person – the individual denied reality if he hid himself in history, or merged himself in a race or a class or a church. This was the meaning of the assertion that subjectivity was truth, that Christianity was not another system of knowledge to be studied, but a paradox, an absurdity, to be believed. The absurd was that eternal truth had come into being in time, that God had come into being, had been born, had grown up, and so forth, precisely like any other individual human being (see *Concluding Unscientific Postscript*, E.T. Princeton 1941, p. 188). Only by becoming a Christian could one 'know' Christianity. Becoming a Christian meant the setting-up in a leap of faith of an existential relationship between the self and the God-Man. This relation to Christ, though passionately inward, did not mean

for Kierkegaard the discovery of an immanent 'ground of being' in the self,
an idea with a long history which Paul Tillich revived in the twentieth
century. That kind of immanent religious consciousness would have seemed
to Kierkegaard only a step towards a truly Christian faith, which he always
described as a relation to that which was outside the anguished, suffering,
consciously sinful self. An absolute, passionately inward devotion to the
Absolute relativized the finite, but it did not relativize the Absolute. And
the end of the relationship was a new creation of the self, a gift of God, and
radically discontinuous with the old.

It is not hard to see why Kierkegaard had little influence on Victorian
theology. He could understand the liberal tradition, but he did not sym-
pathize with it, because its kind of Kantian base excluded the existentialism
which he developed. Nor was he attracted by an orthodox liturgical revival
like Anglo-Catholicism. And while other conservatives, Maurice and Newman for example, wanted to restore the Church, Protestant or Catholic, to
its pre-revolutionary rôle as the source and arbiter of morals, education,
and training in social obedience, Kierkegaard attacked Christendom
because he believed that religious institutions were bound to connive at
social man's desire to replace truly primitive Christianity (which meant
the renunciation of the earthly), with a religion which legitimized the
disappearance of renunciation. More powerful secular movements, such as
nationalism and various forms of socialism, appealed to men as mass in
motion; Kierkegaard could only appeal to individual people's inward
restlessness. Even in the twentieth century, when he became famous as one
of the precursors of existentialism, he was more the subject of academic
theses than of theological attention. Simone Weil was his nearest modern
equivalent, but not his disciple. In both, much more than in any other
theological writers of their period, isolated readers found a passionate
inward grasp of the being of God and the immorality of man.

Roman Catholic theology in the nineteenth century suffered the same
inner conflicts which have just been described in the case of Protestantism,
but the process was complicated by the rapid revival of the papacy as the
centre of Catholic authority after 1815. Nineteenth-century popes sharply
opposed theological liberalism; even Newman's conservatism had a cool
reception in Rome; Pius IX (1846–78) actually tried to strengthen the
position of orthodoxy by making it more explicit. A few theologians might
have ecclesiastical influence, but the reigning pope had power, and this was
used, both at the first Vatican Council, and in the Modernist crisis after
1900, against any attempt to modify the orthodox concept of revelation;
conservatism was distrusted, because its primary appeal to religious
experience was seen as unwise and unnecessary.

The official condemnation of the resolutions of the liberal synod of
Pistoia (1786) has usually been interpreted as the closure of the account
marked Jansenism and Febronianism; in fact, however, the anti-clerical
atmosphere of nineteenth-century north-Italian nationalism may be traced
back partly to the failure of the Enlightenment campaign for ecclesiastical
reform. As a whole, the Roman Church emerged from the Napoleonic wars
weakened in France, Spain and Italy: hence, for example, the French

Catholic demand for the restoration of church property seized during the
Revolution, and for a conscious repudiation of the ideology of the Revolution itself; but neither the property nor the national repentance was really
forthcoming. Theologically, Rome itself continued to assert the traditional
doctrine of the divinely-given authority of the teaching Church. The
seminaries, which had been one of the targets of the synod of Pistoia,
remained isolated in a seventeenth-century intellectual universe long after
1815. Chateaubriand's (1768–1848) romantic invocation of the rôle of
Roman Catholicism in the European past, *Le Génie du Christianisme* (1802),
had no theological force, but the appeal to authority, the authority of the
past, was typical of the Catholic mind at this period. Lamennais' *Essai sur
L'Indifférence en matière de religion* (vol 1, 1817; vol 2, 1820), similarly
urged men to put aside the claims of their own individual reason, and to
trust instead to the general reason, or *sensus communis*, to what humanity,
guided by God, had always understood and believed, a religion which the
Catholicism of Jesus had finally and fully revealed. In the long run
Lamennais substituted the authority of the race for the authority of the
pope, and abandoned Roman Catholicism for the Deism and revolutionary
politics which were already logically implicit in the *Essai*.[1] Those who had
doubted his orthodoxy from the start could argue that they had been
justified; those who suspected J. H. Newman's *Essay on the Development of
Christian Doctrine* (1845) of unsoundness were less evidently proved correct.

In Roman Catholic teaching as it was defined at the commencement of
the nineteenth century revelation was defined as the content of the Old
and New Testaments understood in the medium of tradition and expounded
in the Church, through the Creeds, the Patristic writers, the Councils
(including Trent) and specific papal pronouncements. Nothing could be
added to the basic material, nor could there by any question of any new
divinely revealed material. For the scholastic theologian dogmatic change
took place through the logical elucidation of this original data. Since
Newman was not convinced that theological change or development could
be defended in this way, he needed a theory which would answer the
Protestant assertion that Roman Catholicism had made illegitimate
additions (the Marian theology, for example) to the original deposit of
necessary faith. Once proposed, the theory had also to accommodate the
papal proclamation of the dogma of the immaculate conception of the
Virgin Mary (*Ineffabilis Deus*, 1854), and the first Vatican Council's
definition of the infallibility of the papacy (*Pastor Aeternus*, 1870).

Newman broke with the view that theological development was a matter
of logic. He took as his model the development of an *idea*, and described
the process as the germination, growth and perfection of some living truth
in the minds of men over a sufficient period of time. Put in this way, the
development of the *idea* of Christianity might seem dangerously subjective,
but Newman thought of this essentially divine idea as regulative, living its
own life, gradually excluding false developments and extending itself in the

---

[1] For Lamennais, see the section on *Social Theology*. For the more strictly philosophical
aspects of nineteenth-century French Catholic thought, see *Liberalism and Tradition*,
B. Reardon (1975).

human consciousness. Once again one has the post-Kantian attempt to unite subjective experience with an objective self-giving of the Absolute; Newman tried to weaken the risk of subjectivity by saying that the developmental process took place in the mind of the whole Church, laity included. And there was, in any case, the organ of infallibility which, divinely guided, protected men troubled by the ambiguities of theological discussion, or tempted by the arrogant wilfulness of an unilluminated human reason. As a general defence of the possibility of some kind of doctrinal development the theory was persuasive, especially when Newman spoke of the Church as the most sacred and august of poets;[1] but it offered little help to those who were quite prepared to believe that the dogma of the Assumption of the Virgin had developed historically, being probably unknown before the fourth century, but who interpreted its germination, growth, and perfection as a constant development away from the original idea of Christianity.[2] In such a case, Newman's theory was too elastic to mollify Protestant suspicion, and his emphasis on the need to consult the laity in the process of infallible definition did not seem a significant safeguard. It was hardly surprising that conversations in the 1970s between Anglican and Roman Catholic theologians made no process on subjects like infallibility. Within the Roman Church, however, Newman's view of development became a powerful engine in the hands of those who, without approaching what in Protestant terms would have been a liberal position, wanted to make Roman Catholicism more open to change, and who welcomed the fresh impetus given by the second Vatican Council. Even so, by the 1970s theories of development in general were losing their charm. Coherent versions of human history as guided towards a goal, whether Catholic, Marxist or Protestant, seemed to lack plausibility. The world seemed more as it had seemed to Soeren Kierkegaard, for whom Christ was simply a contemporary, neither developed from the past, nor developing into the future; or to Simone Weil, for whom the apparent momentum of history was a force to resist. Through the eighteenth and nineteenth centuries, justification by development had been a popular move in both conservative and liberal circles; now the idea looked more obviously imposed on the past than derived from it.

Officially, however, the Roman Catholic Church reaffirmed orthodox intransigence under Pius IX, who had suffered from political liberalism in the Roman revolution of 1848–49. In the *Syllabus Errorum* of December, 1864, Pius condemned eighty propositions which he considered typical of the errors of mid-century Italy and Europe in general. The *Syllabus* attracted attention above all because of its famous eightieth condemnation, when Pius denied that he either could or should reconcile himself to, or agree with, progress, liberalism, and civilization as they were then fashionably defined. In Italian terms the *Syllabus* meant that the Pope would not agreed to Piedmontese demands for a secular education system and the

---

[1] J. H. Newman, *Essays Critical and Historical*, vol. 2 (1901), p. 442. Originally written in 1846.

[2] The Assumption was defined *ex cathedra* by Pius XII in 1950 in *Munificentissimus Deus*.

abolition of monasticism, that he would not make peace with the coolly triumphant, anticlerical Cavour. Some interpreters' have said that no wider application existed in Pius' mind, but the decision of the first Vatican Council to proclaim the infallibility of the Pope when speaking *ex cathedra* on matters of faith or morals, put the earlier statement in its proper perspective.

The unification of Italy as a typical modern state underlined the failure of the social and political restoration of 1815; the eighteenth-century campaign for freedom from the Church was still continuing, and with growing success. The new, middle-class states were setting up civil, largely secular education systems and introducing legislation to sanction civil marriage and divorce. The modern state was freeing itself from organized religion, something which Jansenism had not foreseen, and which the ecclesiastics who had believed that they had 'defeated' Jansenism had not foreseen either. In the circumstances, Pius IX's assertion that the Catholic Church and the Papacy were the essential element in western (and by implication, all human) society, was inevitable. In 1864–70 the Pope seemed to be saying that orthodoxy was directly and permanently opposed to human progress in the widest meaning of the words; but the opposition looked natural to Pius because he could not voluntarily accept the reduction of Christianity to one among several religious options, and one to which society no longer admitted any official, absolute obligation. (In fact, of course, many Protestants, in England for example, also resisted every manifestation of the separation of Church and State.) Pius IX was himself personally committed to a papal form of definition of the infallibility of the Church, but he was in any case bound to insist on some kind of declaration of theological *certainty* – not to have done so would have seemed to him a surrender of the Roman Church's theological claim to be the channel and servant of a unique, divine revelation. From the orthodox point of view, infallibility was always involved in the struggle with religious liberalism, and this was just as true in Protestantism as in Catholicism. To agree that religious *certainty* was unavailable, either in terms of religious experience or as dogmatic definition, was to shift the locus of religion from the divine to the human, and to banish doctrines like that of the Trinity to the wilderness of speculation.

Pius IX, that is, was not a 'reactionary' as a theologian; rather, he made it clear that orthodoxy was at risk and had to be defended. He refused any premature surrender of the principle that all human life, individual and corporate, was lived within a hierarchical, divinely ordered structure, within which salvation was thought of as 'coming down from heaven' in the Person of Christ, who took flesh and lived among men, but whose capacity to redeem the human race depended on his being divine. For Christ to be a cosmic saviour he must also be a cosmic figure; humanity alone was not equal to the task of restoring or revealing a world-order on a supernatural scale. It was of the essence of the traditional theology that one be intensely suspicious of any proposal for change which had no better authority than the critical use of the human mind. As far as Pius IX and Pius X (1835–1914, Pope from 1903) were concerned, revelation had been given once and for all in the mission of Christ, and had been given clearly in language which stood for ever immune from historicizing forces. Some kind of development of doctrine was tolerable if it meant no more than building extensions to the system; Catholic Modernism, however, had to be resisted, because it implied that one might pull part of the building down.

It was all the more unfortunate that the precipitating factor in the controversy was the attempt by the liberal Protestant ecclesiastical historian, Adolf Harnack (1851–1930), to tackle the problem of theological change in his very successful book, *What is Christianity?* (1900). Harnack tried to make way for change in a characteristic manner which could be traced back to John Locke and the eighteenth-century reductionists. He dismissed the doctrinal elaboration of Christianity in favour of a minimal, allegedly primitive Christian gospel: 'God the Father, Providence, the position of men as God's children, the infinite value of the human soul, (in these) the whole Gospel is expressed'. He extended the sixteenth-century rejection of medieval theology to cover Protestant classicism as well. Perhaps it was the best that he could do, but one is reminded of Newman's epigram, that many a man would live and die upon a dogma, but no man would be a martyr for a conclusion. And Harnack's conclusion was that neither the gospel as systematic theology, nor the Church as a visible institution, nor the Christological dogma as traditionally received, were really part of Jesus's message: it was a case, Harnack said, not of distortion but of total perversion; Catholicism was superfluous and Protestantism only half-reformed. Harnack's was a brilliant presentation of the liberal view of Christianity as the product of the creative insights of the essentially human moral consciousness of Jesus. Indirectly, of course, Harnack was challenging all theories of development, including Newman's, on the ground that development ought not to have taken place.

This was a traditional Protestant argument, which played an important part in the Reformation, but it left Harnack wide open to the reply of Alfred Loisy (1857–1940, a Catholic biblical scholar, in *The Gospel and the Church* (*L'Évangile et L'Église*, 1902). Loisy said that of course, if one started from an abstract, unreal conception of revelation and dogma, one ended by condemning all the results of Christian reflection on Christianity. Clearly, if the unchangeable essence of the Gospel was simply faith in God the Father, then all the later development of Christianity, in doctrine, ecclesiastical order and liturgy, became a vast aberration. However, quite apart from the fact that the Gospel could not be reduced to such a simple faith, it was absurd to suppose that the proclamation of the Gospel could either remain unchanged, or be regarded as unchangeable: Christian doctrinal development was bound to take place, and was therefore legitimate in principle. Taken as a whole, development had served the Gospel, which would not have survived as a rarefied essence but which, perpetually translated into living doctrine, had gone on living through these doctrines, a result which legitimized development as a matter of fact.

The strength of Loisy's position in relation to Harnack, though not in relation to Catholic orthodoxy, was that he was prepared to distinguish between the overall effects of change, which he was ready to defend, and particular instances of development which he might regard as regrettable or mistaken. But while this flexibility made his conception of development more sophisticated than Newman's, it brought him into conflict with Rome. A small group of Catholic intellectuals, including Loisy, the philosopher Maurice Blondel (1861–1949), Lucien Laberthonnière (1860–1932), George Tyrrell (1861–1909) and Friedrich von Hügel (1852–1925) all shared a common disapproval of the intransigeance with which Catholic orthodoxy faced the modern world. Their agreement did not go much further, and it is an exaggeration to speak of a 'Modernist movement'; neither Blondel nor von Hügel, for example, was as committed to the need for theological change as were Loisy and Tyrrell, though both were impressed by the achievements of nineteenth-century Protestant biblical scholarship.

By 1902, in fact, Loisy had already reached the furthest point of the developmental argument. The earlier dogmas, he said, were rooted in the preaching and ministry of Christ and in the experience of the Church; they found their development in the history of Christianity and in theological reflection, and it could not have been otherwise. And what was no less natural was that creeds and dogmatic definitions should be *en rapport* with the general state of human knowledge at the time and the social context in which they were drawn up. It followed, however, that any considerable change in the state of knowledge would make necessary a fresh interpretation of the original formulae, and such a change had been taking place steadily since the beginning of the eighteenth century. One had now to distinguish between the material sense of the formulae – the sense in which they had been *en rapport* with the current ideas of the Ancient World into which Jesus was born – and their fundamental religious meaning, which could still be reconciled with modern views of existence and the nature of things.[1] 'Only truth is immutable', Loisy wrote, 'but not the image of truth in our minds. Faith holds to this unchanging truth by means of formulae which are inevitably inadequate, capable of improvement, and consequently alterable . . . The Church does not require faith in its formulae as though they were the adequate expression of absolute truth, but presents them as the least imperfect expression of the truth which is morally possible.'[2]

It was not surprising that Loisy was felt to have gone too far, and that the anti-Modernist Decree, *Lamentabili* (1907), specifically condemned Loisy's historical relativism, rejecting, for example, the proposition that some articles of the Apostles' Creed (Loisy had instanced the descent of Christ into Hell) did not have the same meaning for twentieth-century Christians as they had had for Christians in the primitive period. Pius X wanted to lay down, not only that the original dogmatic language must be retained, but that the original intention of the words (about which the authors of the encyclical apparently had no problem) must also be accepted. In *Christianity at the Cross-Roads* (1909), actually published after his death, Tyrrell, who had learned from Loisy to see the gospels in eschatological terms, attacked such theological immobilism with specific reference to Jesus himself. What, Tyrrell asked, were the categories and concepts of Jesus to

[1] Alfred Loisy, *L'Evangile et L'Eglise* (1902), pp. 161–65.
[2] *ib.* pp. 166, 174.

men now? Were they to frame their minds to that of a first-century Jewish
carpenter for whom (the echo of Nietzsche was obvious) more than half the
world and nearly the whole of its history did not exist; who cared nothing
for art or science or history or politics or nine-tenths of the interests of
humanity, but solely for the Kingdom of God and its righteousness? It was
the spirit of Jesus that mattered, not the religious ideas and apocalyptic
imagery which were that spirit's inadequate embodiment.[1]

In such an utterance Tyrrell rejected the conservative Catholic concept
of development (that theological ideas could grow, but had always to
remain consistent with their past). The view of change which he was
advocating (that when theology grew it cast off its past as part of the
process) cut the ground from under the liberal Protestant idea of development as well. In a choice which ranged over Strauss, Renan, Nietzsche,
Arnold, Weiss, Liddon and Loisy, the 'spirit of Jesus' became indefinable.
Tyrrell died in conflict with the official Church, Loisy withdrew after ex-
communication in 1908; it was not surprising that von Hügel gave up a
struggle for which he had no intellectual enthusiasm – he was not committed
to a 'modernist' theological view, but only to a campaign for freer research
and discussion, and this Pius X would not tolerate.

In Catholic terms, this left obedience to the Church as the channel and
interpreter of revelation as the only resource, and Pius XII was to reiterate
this position as late as 1950 in his encyclical, *Humani Generis*. Modernism
was not really vindicated until the second Vatican Council (1962–65). The
controversial *Declaration on Religious Freedom* contained the conclusion:
'It is therefore in accord with the nature of faith that in matters religious
every manner of coercion on the part of men should be excluded.'[2] This
statement reversed the traditional teaching of the Roman Church on
religious liberty, and indirectly repudiated the *Syllabus of Errors*. It could
not be squared very convincingly with Newman's view of development,
because the jettisoning of the past involved a discontinuity which amounted
to contradiction. This willingness to go beyond the possibilities of theological development by slow, consistent aggregation, and to accept that
contradiction might be the result of sudden but nevertheless valid, radical
religious change, was the core of Modernism as Loisy and Tyrrell understood it. And when the Declaration began by saying that a sense of the
dignity of the human person had been impressing itself more and more
deeply on the consciousness of contemporary man, it was pointing, as
Loisy had pointed, to the importance of the human cultural background of
theological statements. Historically, the Declaration reflected the emergence
of the United States as a Catholic power.

Any attempt to assess the significance of the second Vatican Council
would still be premature, but theologically, the significant element seemed
to be the recognition of co-existence as intellectual and ecclesiastical
possibility. Broadly, the Council affirmed: the co-existence of the Roman

---

[1] G. Tyrrell, *Christianity at the Cross-Roads* (3 ed., 1910), p. 270.
[2] W. M. Abbott, ed., *The Documents of Vatican II* (New York, 1966), p. 690. One of the
principal authors of the Declaration was an American Jesuit, John Courtney Murray
(1904–67).

Church with other Churches and with secular political philosophies like Marxism; the co-existence of the idea of revelation as the unique self-disclosure of God in Christianity with science (as in biology, where conflict between the magisterium and Catholic biologists has been reduced to a minimum);[1] and co-existence of the traditional dogmatic system, especially where the doctrine of Christ is concerned, with great practical freedom for Catholic biblical scholars.

---

[1] See Wolfhart Pannenberg, *Theology and the Philosophy of Science* (1976), for the most exhaustive recent attempt to examine the 'scientific' status of revelation. For Catholic teaching on evolution, see K. Rahner, *Hominisation* (1965).

III

THE DOCTRINE OF THE CHURCH IN
THE WHOLE PERIOD

Two topics require special consideration in this discussion of modern theology. One is the doctrine of the Church, the other is what may be called social theology, the analysis of the relations between Church and society. In the case of the doctrine of the Church, the nineteenth and twentieth centuries have seen an astonishing variety of ideas, ranging from defences of the highest views of Papal supremacy to the conclusion that one may dispense with the Church altogether. The ecumenical movement has also affected the theological description of the Church. As for social theology, the nineteenth century witnessed a gradual but drastic revolution in theological opinion, the abandonment of the ancient western view that society already expressed the divine will and ought not to be radically changed, and the adoption of the view that society was necessarily in permanent flux and that theology must come to terms with a perpetually altering social structure. We shall examine the history of the doctrine of the Church first.

One may distinguish between the immediate social situation which underlies and explains the formation of a particular doctrine of the Church and the way in which this doctrine is then established within the intellectual tradition and discussed by later theologians in an essentially abstract manner which divorces the theological definitions from their origins. Thus any discussion of the fate of the doctrine of the Church in the eighteenth century must come to terms with the Methodist movement because the Methodists represented the obvious eighteenth-century challenge to accepted ways of thinking about ecclesiastical institutions. John Wesley's basic principle was that dogma took precedence over institutions. The purpose of ecclesiastical institutions was primarily to guard purity of dogma, to organize evangelism and to foster the converts. Existing eighteenth-century Anglican institutions, including the episcopate, were theoretically adequate to do this and might therefore be accepted and obeyed as long as they were faithful to their responsibilities, but if the existing institutions neither ensured purity of doctrine nor evangelized in terms of it, but tolerated a clergy which Wesley, in his sharper mood, could dismiss as ignorant of doctrine and idle in evangelism, then one had both the duty and the right to form new institutions.

Wesley did not regard this as involving schism; he neither unchurched the Church of England nor intended to set up a new national Church. To argue as to whether Wesley himself did or did not intend his followers to separate from the Church of England is to miss the point. He meant them to use Wesleyan institutions to guard and spread the Wesleyan interpretation of the Anglican tradition as contained in the Homilies and the Articles – and he believed the Wesleyan interpretation of these to be the 'pure' one, whose preservation was all important as against either the true High Church or Evangelical Anglican interpretations – until the Establishment reformed itself along similar lines, when the Methodist institutions might dissolve themselves. Wesley did not suppose that he was laying the foundations of permanent institutions which contained the absolute truth in themselves, as had earlier non-episcopal Protestants from the Society of Friends to the Presbyterians; but he thought of himself as creating temporary institutions, pragmatically designed and intended to shelter doctrines which were absolutely true. It is obvious, however, that John Wesley did not consider that episcopacy was one of these eternal truths or he could not have acted as he did. Nor can his behaviour be squared with the theology of obedience to ecclesiastical authority which John Henry Newman taught in his Roman Catholic days. Wesley was practising rather than advocating a theology of pragmatic disobedience. It is interesting to compare Wesley's position with the argument which Newman advanced in the *Apologia*, the *locus classicus* of ecclesiastical obedience:

> There is a time for everything, and many a man desires a reformation of an abuse, or the fuller development of a doctrine, or the adoption of a particular policy, but forgets to ask himself whether the right time for it has come; and, knowing that there is no one who will be doing anything towards its accomplishment in his own lifetime unless he does it himself, he will not listen to the voice of authority, and he spoils a good work in his own century, in order that another man, as yet unborn, may not have the opportunity of bringing it happily to perfection in the next. He may seem to the world to be nothing else than a bold champion for the truth and a martyr to free opinion, when he is just one of those persons whom the competent authority ought to silence; and, though the case may not fall within that subject-matter in which that authority is infallible, or the formal conditions of the exercise of the gift may be wanting, it is clearly the duty of authority to act vigorously in the case.[1]

Methodism, however, was not limited by such subtle considerations. And one reason for this may also have been that Wesley's actions and their theological justification could serve as a rationalization of a social schism which had developed in English society in the seventeenth century. This social division had been reflected in the formation of the Puritan movement in the Church of England and in the formation of the Baptist, Independent and Presbyterian local churches, but these had declined as a result of defeat in the Civil War and its aftermath. The spread of the Wesleyan societies was in many ways a reassertion in the religious sphere of the continuing social divisions of the country (which were not the same as the class-structure which grew up in the nineteenth century). John Wesley's attitude to religious institutions fitted pragmatically into this situation.

[1] J. H. Newman, *Apologia Pro Sua Vita* (M. J. Svaglic ed. 1967), p. 232.

For social and economic reasons Methodism proved unable to maintain a single set of institutions either in Britain or in the United States in the nineteenth century. A period of progressive fragmentation which lasted until the setting up of the Salvation Army in the 1870s (the teaching about holiness which distinguished the Army in its early days had American Methodist roots) deprived the Methodists of any great influence on the ecclesiology of the mainstream Churches, all of which remained committed officially to more absolute theories of the Church's nature. The pragmatic tradition survived in Methodism, however, as for example in this modern American Methodist statement on the doctrine of the Church:

> There remains a deep, almost instinctive awareness among us that our foremost and final justification for being the Church that we are is still precisely the same as the justification for our having first been an evangelical order within the ecclesia Anglicana – namely, Christianity in dead earnest, distinguished chiefly in our evangelical concern for the Christian mission, witness, nurture – 'holiness of heart and life'. I cannot myself point to any contemporary formulation or formula that I would acknowledge as the Methodist doctrine of the Church . . . The drift of these comments is that Methodism has never lost the *essence* of a *functional* doctrine of the Church but that, by the same token, it has never developed – on its own and for itself – the full panoply of bell, book and candle that goes with being a 'proper' Church properly self-understood. This makes us une église manquée, theoretically and actually.[1]

Outler uses the word 'evangelism' in a wide sense, so that it included Wesley's idea of doctrinal fidelity. In the twentieth century, of course, the suggestion that the Gospel is readily and absolutely definable is much more questionable than it was in the eighteenth century and does not provide an easy way of determining the Church-status of a particular religious body. It may seem, nevertheless, one of the tragedies of the historical development of the ecumenical movement that this pragmatic, or functional, attitude to the visible Church dropped so far into the background in the course of the nineteenth century. The renewed emphasis on the ecclesiological centrality of episcopacy which stemmed from Tractarianism retarded the advance of ecumenism without securing corresponding pragmatic advantages. John Wesley's view of the Church ruled out the idea that episcopacy was of the *esse* of the Church.

In the eighteenth century as a whole the doctrine of the Church did not attract much attention in Church of England and Roman Catholic circles. The inherited ecclesiastical structures were taken for granted except when at the political level the interests of Church and State clashed, as they did, for example, in the Austria of Joseph II. As long as ecclesiastical leaders could take it for granted that Christendom still existed, as long as they could assume that people generally accepted the partnership of Church and State as the divinely ordained pattern for the government of mankind, they did not greatly worry if men often ignored the ideal in practice. It was

[1] D. Kirkpatrick, ed., *The Doctrine of the Church* (1964), p. 25.

characteristic of nineteenth-century ecclesiology that theoretical defences of this allegedly organic relationship continued to appear in England, where the establishment of the Church of England was challenged, modified, but never finally abolished. S. T. Coleridge and F. D. Maurice both wrote from this point of view. Church establishment, in various forms, had been the standard form, and it was one of the significant changes of the period that all over Europe, in Roman Catholic as well as in Protestant countries, the State moved to bring the union to an end, setting up secular institutions for education, for instance, and for marriage, and permitting an increasing degree of religious competition, which in the past had been regarded as injurious to the State's own interests. In the United States of America establishment did not long survive the Revolution. It was one of the profound insights of the Danish theologian, Soren Kierkegaard, that he recognized not only that Christendom had collapsed but also that one could not make a successful programme out of a desire to restore the religious *ancien régime*. Many who admitted the futility of dreaming of a political restoration still hoped for a religious one.

The situation differed radically from what had happened in England in the seventeenth century when two powerful groups had fought for supremacy *within* the Church of England, both taking the idea of Christendom for part of the divine revelation. In the nineteenth century European states shifted rapidly towards a position of greater independence – it does not make much difference whether one calls this secularization or not. Broadly speaking, only a minority of right-wing, normally conservative political groups struggled very hard against this process. It was this political withdrawal from the old compact which compelled theologians to re-examine the doctrine of the Church, and the pre-occupation has continued. To speak, as has sometimes been done, of a theological rediscovery of the doctrine of the Church in the 1930s is misleading: the doctrine was central to Victorian theological perplexities, because after the French Revolution no one knew what the rôle of the Church was in a modern state.

Indeed, the modern ecumenical movement partly originated in the anxiety of church leaders to replace the vanished social order in which the Churches had played an accepted part with a united ecclesiastical institution capable of holding its own as an independent structure with the increasingly independent and secular state. The question which John Henry Newman, then still Anglican, asked in the first of the famous Oxford *Tracts for the Times* (1834) was therefore already in dead earnest:

> Should the Government and the country so far forget their God as to cast off the Church, to deprive it of its temporal honours and substance, on what will you rest the claim of respect and attention which you make upon your flocks? Hitherto you have been upheld by your birth, your education, your wealth, your connexions – should these secular advantages cease, on what must Christ's ministers depend?

Precisely the same problem confronted the Roman Catholic Church in France after the Revolution of 1830 had replaced the restored but un-improved Bourbons with a July monarchy which carefully avoided any open identification of itself with the Catholic Church, the traditional spiritual expression of the ancient French monarchy. There the suddenly inspired Lamennais took the opposite, liberal solution which Newman never seriously considered. In Italy, the question raised itself in the still sharper form of the Papal knowledge that Italian nationalism must sooner or later challenge the Church's temporal power in central Italy, where the Papal states, to complicate matters, were not conspicuously well-governed, and that the city of Rome itself had little enthusiasm for the Pope as a ruler. The alternative to the old alliance did not seem as simple then as necessity has made it seem since. 'We know,' Newman wrote, 'how miserable is the state of religious bodies not supported by the State. Look at the Dissenters on all sides of you and you will see that their ministers, depending simply upon the people, become the *creatures* of the people. Are you content that this should be your case? Alas, can a greater evil befall Christians than for their teachers to be guided by them, instead of guiding? Is it not our very office to *oppose* the world? Can we then allow ourselves to *court* it? To preach smooth things and prophesy deceits? To make the way of life easy for the rich and indolent and to bribe the humbler classes by excitements and strong intoxicating doctrine? Surely it must not be so – and the question recurs – on what are we to rest our authority when the State deserts us?'[1]

The issue was not one, in other words, of establishment or disestablishment. As such, the latter would bring no authority. The British state, while not actually disentangling itself entirely from the Anglican Church in England, was becoming more independent in spirit. If an act of disestablishment were passed through parliament it would be an act of recognition, not an act of revolution. A social order was falling apart, and Newman argued the case for a doctrine of the Church which would guarantee spiritual power both to the institution and to its ministers. 'Christ has not left his Church without claim of his own upon the attention of men. Surely not. Hard master he cannot be, to bid us oppose the world, yet give us no credentials for so doing.' Newman rejected in advance some of the solutions popular with his contemporaries. 'There are some who rest their divine mission upon their own unsupported assertion; others, who rest it upon their popularity; others, on their success; others, who rest it upon their temporal distinction. This last case has, perhaps, been too much our own; I fear we have neglected the real ground on which our authority is built, our apostolical descent.' His explanation of 'apostolical descent' showed why the idea attracted him. 'We have been,' he said, 'born not of blood, nor of the will of the flesh, nor of the will of man, but of God. The Lord Jesus Christ gave his Spirit to his Apostles; they in turn laid their hands on those who should succeed them; and these again on others; and so the sacred gift had been handed down to our present Bishops who have appointed us to be their assistants, and in some sense representatives.'[2]

Such an assertion – for it was in fact simply an assertion – placed the origin and authority of the Church (at any rate of the Anglican part of it, which was all that Newman was concerned with at that particular moment)

---

[1] *Tracts for the Times*, 1 (J. H. Newman), 1834.
[2] *ib.*

beyond the power of secular institutions which no longer cared to claim a divine origin and authority for themselves. In the past politicians had assumed that the Church was a necessary and useful element in human society, even if they had not embraced the high doctrine of the Counter-Reformation, exemplified in the treatises of Robert Bellarmine (1542–1621), and sometimes repeated in Roman Catholic circles even in the mid-twentieth century, that a civil state which acknowledged the laws of the Roman Catholic Church was a useful element or function within the mystical body of Christ which formed the primary notion and stuff of society. The disintegration of this theoretical unity, however regarded, of which Newman was certainly aware (as was Kierkegaard), meant that to survive the hostility or indifference of the nineteenth-century state, itself a child of the Enlightenment in many ways, the Church must claim a spiritual origin and an authority derived directly from Christ himself.

Here episcopal ordination came in as a convenient way of giving concreteness to the assertion of spiritual independence – 'if we trace back the power of ordination from hand to hand of course we shall come to the Apostles at last – we know we do, as a plain historical fact'.[1] This assertion, however, which Newman made with a fine disregard of the historical problems involved, was about the basis of the Church, not about the natural succession of bishops. In the Eleventh Tract Newman, anxious to conciliate, laboured to show that the Bible pointed to God's having set up a permanent, visible Church which Christians (as a general rule) were bound to join, so that to believe in Christ was not a mere opinion or secret conviction, but a social and even political principle; but the biblical evidence, like the episcopal succession, was essentially corroborative as far as Newman was concerned. His final withdrawal from the Anglican communion showed that for him the Anglican episcopal succession had not proved able to maintain a close enough continuity with that Primitive Christianity which had become his fundamental standard. It was the inner logic of the historical situation in the nineteenth century which compelled him to seek such an absolute authority for the Church, as was clear from his description of the world order in the *Apologia*:

What a scene, what a prospect, does the whole of Europe present at this day. And not only Europe, but every government and every civilisation throughout the world, which is under the influence of the European mind. Especially, for it most concerns us, how sorrowful, in the view of religion, even taken in its most elementary, most attenuated form, is the spectacle presented to us by the educated intellect of Europe, France and Germany. Lovers of their country and their race, religious men, external to the Catholic Church, have attempted various expedients to arrest fierce wilful human nature in its onward course and to bring it into subjection. The necessity of some form of religion for the interests of humanity, has been generally acknowledged; but where was the concrete representation of things invisible which would have the force and the toughness necessary to be the breakwater

[1] *ib.*

against the deluge? Three centuries ago the establishment of religion
. . . was generally adopted as the best expedient for the purpose in
those countries which separated from the Catholic Church; and for a
long time it was successful; but now the crevices of those establishments
are admitting the enemy.[1]

It is significant that in the United States of America, which had abandoned the principle of church establishment, which kept up a kind of
conscientious objection to the *ancien régime*, and where the influence of
organized Christianity had come to rely in the early nineteenth century on
the work of the revivalist tradition, Anglicanism produced, at about the
same time as Anglo-Catholicism appeared in England, but without any
obvious English prompting, a movement very similar to Tractarianism and
committed to much the same view of the nature of the Church. Those who,
because of their inheritance of the habit of close association with the state,
saw more clearly the change that was taking place, were the most determined to find a supernatural sanction for the Church's visible being, a
sanction which, however dependent on the Bible for its intellectual backing,
might also serve as an answer to German historical-critical reassessments
of the Scriptures. The authority of the Church, established outside the realm
permitted to human reason, might support or replace the weakened
authority of the Book. It was significant that Kierkegaard, who was
accustomed to a state Church in Lutheran Denmark, came to speak of
religious authority as to be found only in a divine invasion of the present
age, when God chose to reveal himself, however darkly, through a particular
individual. Kierkegaard, that is, also tried to locate authority beyond the
power and influence of nineteenth-century secularizing society, whether it
was represented by the political state or the philosophical critic.

Following such a line of thought, it was not unnatural that Newman
should, in his Roman Catholic phase, defend the concept of the Church's
infallibility, as he did in the *Apologia*, where he related the idea to the
despairing picture of human culture which has already been quoted:

> Supposing it, then, to be the Will of the Creator to interfere in human
> affairs, and to make provision for retaining in the world a knowledge
> of Himself, so definite and distinct as to be proof against the energy of
> human scepticism, in such a case – I am far from saying that there was
> no other way – but there is nothing to surprise the mind if He should
> think fit to introduce a power into the world invested with the pre-
> rogative of infallibility in religious matters. Such a provision would be
> a direct, immediate, active and prompt means of withstanding the
> difficulty . . . And thus I am brought to speak of the Church's infalli-
> bility as a provision adapted by the mercy of the Creator to preserve
> religion in the world, and to restrain that freedom of thought, which
> of course in itself is one of the greatest of our natural gifts, and to
> rescue it from its own suicidal excesses . . . a power, possessed of
> infallibility in religious teaching, is happily adapted to be a working
> instrument, in the course of human affairs, for smiting hard and

[1] J. H. Newman, *Apologia*, p. 219.

throwing back the immense energy of the aggressive, capricious, untrustworthy intellect . . .[1]

And since an infallibility which never pronounced judgement would be little better than no infallibility at all, this argument – for men like Pius IX shared Newman's dread of the immense energy of the untrustworthy intellect – led on either to a declaration of Papal infallibility, as happened at the first Vatican Council (1870) or to some kind of committee infallibility (usually on the basis of the episcopate), an idea which has sometimes been mentioned in twentieth-century ecumenical and Roman Catholic discussion. It must be realized, however, that Newman himself did not think of papal infallibility as simply the individual activity of a particular Pope who weighed up the evidence on a point concerning faith or morals and gave an *ex cathedra* decision. He thought of infallibility as a process, which might take place over a long period and involve a conflict between ecclesiastical authority and reason, so that when authority finally felt called on to pronounce a decision, the decision had already been reached within the proper scope of reason. The wilfulness, scepticism and destructiveness of reason dominated the society which surrounded the Church; domiciled within the Church, however, human reason regained its purpose and moved towards truth. And in religious issues part of the truth, for reason, consisted in recognizing the limits of mere rationalism. Reason was not infallible, but infallibility did not destroy the freedom of the intellect.

Newman apart, however, the importance of the Anglo-Catholic movement in the development of modern ecumenicalism has been under-estimated because of the intransigent rejection of the ministries of non-episcopal Churches which was one of its first products. Speaking of ordination in the apostolic succession in *Tract One* Newman said that 'we must necessarily conclude none to be *really* ordained who have not been *thus* ordained', and the point once made remained a thorn in the side of the Protestant ecumenical movement. One has to view this in perspective. When Anglo-Catholicism gave an official description of its position in 1947 in the report entitled *Catholicity*, the authors said that 'the Anglican knows that wherever he worships throughout the Anglican Communion he will find the Holy Scriptures read and the public worship conducted in the vulgar tongue; he will find the historic Creeds recited alike in the rite of Holy Baptism and in the offices; he will find the Sacrament of Confirmation administered by the Bishop; and he will know that the celebrant at the Eucharist is a priest whom a Bishop, standing in the Apostolic Succession, has ordained. These things may be differently valued by churchmen, and even by theologians, but it is upon the constancy of these things in one single pattern that the unity of the Anglican communion rests, with the frank conviction that some parts of the pattern which are not held to be of the *esse* by some Anglicans are held to be of the *esse*, with conviction, by others.'[2]

In fact, the Anglo-Catholic emphasis on the origin and essence of the

---

[1] *ib.* pp. 219–20.
[2] *Catholicity*, A Report presented to the Archbishop of Canterbury (1947), pp. 55–6.

Church as a supernatural body which should be visibly and episcopally one was to penetrate Protestantism – and Anglo-Catholicism was 'protestant', however much some Anglo-Catholics disliked the label – more and more in the later nineteenth century. This influence was increased by the way in which the Oxford movement assisted in the professionalization of the clergy. As one Anglican observer, C. A. Whittuck, said (in 1893), clergy of the Tractarian pattern sought 'to eliminate from their lives any tendency to unclericalise themselves in their intercourse with other men'.[1] The ministerial training seminary, whose introduction throughout Protestantism was a marked feature of nineteenth-century religious history, was conceived as an instrument for the spiritual and professional rather than intellectual formation of the ministry. There was resistance from the older school, 'happy', as Whittuck said, 'in their intercourse with the mixed life of this world',[2] but a revolution slowly took place which implied a new theology of the ministry. The mid-twentieth-century appetite for what was called a 'secular theology', or even, in Harvey Cox's phrase, a 'political theology', implied a reaction against this ascetic view of the priesthood and against the concept of the Church linked with it. Perhaps one may see here the terminus of a mood which had begun as far back as the 1830s.

If eighteenth-century theologians had been able to assume the traditional idea of the Church, whether Roman or Protestant, and had defended the general truth of Christianity rather than the specific doctrine of the Church, nineteenth-century theologians felt obliged to defend the existence and nature of the Church because of the collapse of Christendom, the expansion of the modern state, and increasing criticism of the Church as an institution (and a property-holding institution at that) in human society. It is interesting here to compare Newman's solution of the problem with that of Lamennais, the French Catholic theologian who withdrew into a romantic humanism in the 1830s – he was the arch-example of the impatient, disobedient reformer whom Newman so distrusted. Newman's doctrine of the Church in the 1830s was very much a theoretical one; he did not, as an Anglican, campaign for disestablishment, or do anything to weaken in England the surviving outward signs of the old agreement between state and Church, nor did he seek to organize the Anglican Church to oppose the state: his normal target was the ecclesiastical authorities. Lamennais, on the other hand, perhaps more acutely conscious of the socio-political changes which were taking place in Europe, actually wanted the Roman Church to accentuate the breach with the French monarchy which had opened in 1830, to abandon the principle that the state ought to support the Church with all the means at its power. He wanted to loosen as quickly as possible the ties between French Catholicism and the monarchical world with which the French episcopal hierarchy continued to identify itself long after the Revolution of 1789. Newman wanted a spiritual declaration of independence from the state, coupled with some effort to prevent the state's further secularization – he was still committed psychologically to the idea of Christendom. Lamennais accepted as inevitable the progressive

[1] C. A. Whittuck, *The Church of England and Recent Religious Thought* (1893), p. 24.
[2] *ib.* p. 26.

dechristianization of the state; he wanted to make the Church politically as well as spiritually free so that it need not oppose but might even enter into a democratic system, the form of the new society which he believed was forming. Newman's doctrine of the Church was ascetic; the supernatural society existed on earth in time as the embodiment of grace both offered in the sacraments and received in the saints. Lamennais, like Kierkegaard in Denmark at the same period (1830–50) lacked Newman's willingness to discern such a Church in the existing pattern of institutions and thought that there must be an ecclesiastical revolution as a complement to the socio-political revolution which was still developing.

By the 1850s, in other words, lines had been laid down which led to the twentieth-century controversy about the nature of the Church and the ecumenical movement. From John Wesley, who believed in Protestant orthodoxy without hesitation but who was eighteenth-century enough to remain unimpressed by traditional institutions, there derived an ecclesiastical pragmatism in which doctrinal fidelity took precedence over ecclesiastical form. From the Tractarians stemmed both the idea of corporate visible unity, as distinct from the common nineteenth-century view that Church unity meant the voluntary association for common purposes of individual Christians without any question of organic union – and the stickiness about episcopal ordination which marred modern gropings after unity. From Catholic liberals like Lamennais there followed a view, not unlike John Wesley's, that religious institutions were a means, not an end in themselves: 'I am a follower of Christ, not of the Church', Lamennais said, rejecting all theological schemes which fused the two; but Lamennais also insisted that the vital factor was neither episcopacy nor doctrine but the European cultural revolution, an attitude which was to lead to the Catholic Modernist movement (1900), and the efforts of the French worker-priests to transform French Catholicism after the Second World War. In the 1960s the second Vatican Council reflected a movement away from Newman's emphasis on Christendom and institutional tradition, without any substantial movement in Lamennais' direction.

This summary does not exhaust the creativity of nineteenth-century theology. There was also the strongly individualistic attitude of Soeren Kierkegaard, who thought that the Church (epitomized for him in the state Church of Denmark) was a limiting factor on the chances of Christianity's survival. Whereas Newman in thinking about Christendom looked back to the old order as a lost but loved ideal, and Lamennais wanted to reconstitute it on a democratic basis so that the religion of the state was a religion which emanated from the people instead of being imposed upon them from above, Kierkegaard used the term 'Christendom' as one of abuse. The famous *Attack upon Christendom* (1854–55) was a formal repudiation of the religious results of the *ancien régime*. 'Every effort to bring about a Christian state and a Christian nation is *eo ipse* unchristian, anti-christian', he said, 'for every such effort is only possible in virtue of a reduction of the definition of a Christian, and is therefore against Christianity, and tending to establish the false claim that we are all Christians, and that it is therefore very easy to be Christian. In the New Testament Christianity is the performance of

"duties towards God", and now it has long been decided that there are
really no duties towards God – yet we are Christians, and in fact this is
precisely what constitutes Christendom.'[1]

Kierkegaard felt that Protestantism as institutionalized Christianity had
sacrificed the Gospel to the exigencies of human nature:

> If Protestantism is to be anything but a necessary corrective at a given
> moment, is it not really man's revolt against Christianity? If Christian-
> ity is to be proclaimed as it essentially is in the Gospels, proclaimed as,
> and actually being, imitation or following, sheer suffering, groaning
> and lamentation, heightened by a background of judgement in which
> every word must be accounted for, then it is a terrible series of
> suffering, *angst*, and trembling. Indeed, yes. But where do we read in
> the Gospels that God wishes this earthly existence to be otherwise?
> What human nature constantly aims at, on the other hand, is peace,
> *nil beatum nisi quietum*, peace to carry on with finite things, to enjoy
> life here. Is not Protestantism then man's revolt against Christianity?
> We will and must have peace – peace for Christianity. So we turn the
> whole of Christianity around, and out of the terrible pessimism which
> Christianity is in the New Testament we obtain an insipid optimism . . .[2]

This passage showed the influence of the *zeitgeist*, for Kierkegaard's
description of Protestantism as a system for taking the sting out of
Christianity was remarkably similar to John Keble's quite independent
Anglo-Catholic criticism of the doctrine of justification by faith as practised
in the Anglican Evangelicalism of his day as meaning self-justification – as
though, Keble said, a man failed entirely to see the seriousness of sin but
simply paused and apologized to God, and passed on convinced that he
would be saved in the end by his faith alone. All this concerns the doctrine
of the Church because Kierkegaard regarded the Church as the set of
institutions through which the Gospel had been made impotent; Keble, on
the other hand, turned, like Newman, *to* the Church as the only possible
objective defence against what seemed to him the corrupt subjectivity of
popular Protestantism. The Danish theologian's essential pietism came out
in his horror of objectivity, his certainty that religion exists only in the
personal relation between God and the believer: 'Nothing is more dangerous
than that something which should be practised is transformed into learned
knowledge'. At times the Church seemed to exist for him simply as an
intrusive temptation to be satisfied with an objective, philosophical
religion, which he symbolized as reliance on the fact of infant baptism. He
was aware that Luther had attained salvation after 'a score of years filled
with fear and trembling and temptation', but he found in nineteenth-
century Lutheranism only the transformation of Luther's experience into
a bourgeois non-event, so that membership of the state Lutheran Church
meant security and complacency instead of fear and trembling.

> Christianity is so arranged that it is related to the individual. And it is
> in this that the immense ideality and effort of being a Christian

[1] S. Kierkegaard, *The Last Years* (ed. R. G. Smith, 1965), p. 334.
[2] *ib.* pp. 49–50.

consists, in being related to God as an individual, not protected by any abstraction, which, if you like, softens the blow . . . But what everything human aims at is to be quit of God. This is the common aim. The method is then twofold . . . The first way is to rebel against God, or to deny that there is a God. I do not speak of this. The second way is the more refined. It is under the pretext of zeal for God and the things of God to place an abstraction between God and oneself. Such an abstraction is the 'Church'. Men have struck on the idea of turning it into a person, and by first speaking of it spiritually as a person, about its birth and the course of its life and so on, in the end grow accustomed to identifying the Church with the Christians – and there are no Christians in any sense but this . . .[1]

Once again one notes the power of the *zeitgeist* and the English parallel, for Benjamin Jowett of Balliol, the leading Anglican liberal theologian, confided to his notebooks in the mid-nineteenth century the dismissal of the Church as 'a figment of theologians'. Of course Kierkegaard wrote as the pietist for whom only absolutely certain (and yet always absolutely uncertain) salvation would do; as the pietist whom the Church in history always horrified by its social and political behaviour; as the pietist for whom the Church, if it must be there at all, must be as a common subjectivity united in a common apprehension of the mercy of God in Christ. But he was also more serious than orthodox commentators have sometimes suggested in his analysis of the Church as the vehicle of human, not supernatural religion. He did not really accept the 'Church' as a supernatural guide, or regard it as the natural source of religious authority in the present world. If one compares him with a late nineteenth-century liberal Protestant theologian like Harnack, for example, Kierkegaard's individualism seems deeply religious and Harnack's much more political:

as Protestants we ought to know that we belong, not to an 'invisible' Church, but to a spiritual community which disposes of the forces pertaining to spiritual communities; a spiritual community resting on earth, but reaching to the Eternal . . . This community embraces Protestants inside and outside Germany, Lutherans, Calvinists, and adherents of other denominations. In all of them, as far as they are earnest Christians, there lives a common element, and this element is of infinitely greater importance and value than all their differences . . . And when we are reproached with our divisions and told that Protestantism has as many doctrines as heads, we reply, 'So it has, but we do not wish it otherwise; on the contrary, we want still more freedom, still greater individuality in utterance and doctrine . . . we are well aware that in the interests of order and instruction outward and visible communities must arise . . . but we do not hang our hearts upon them, for they may exist today and tomorrow give place . . . to new organizations; let anyone who has such a Church have it as though he had it not . . .[2]

[1] *ib.* p. 297.
[2] A. Harnack, *What is Christianity?* (ET E. B. Saunders, 1900), pp. 274–77.

Harnack's anti-dogmatic liberalism led him on to an individualistic
praise of freedom which was attractive to many in the late nineteenth
century, but was anathema to Kierkegaard, whose subjectivism was a
subjectivism of religious experience, of encounter with God as the Absolute
who made absolute demands for obedience upon his creatures; Harnack's
was more of a revolt against absolutes, on the ground that the individual
Christian must choose for himself what he would or would not believe,
because there were no trustworthy sources of absolute authority in the
finite world. Harnack's liberal idea of the Church conceded that institutions
were necessary for practical purposes but sought to deny them power over
the life of the individual; his position depended upon the assumption that
the Gospel was 'so simple, so divine, and therefore so truly human, as to be
most certain of being understood when it is left entirely free'.[1] Kierkegaard
started from the opposite assumption that men did not want to be
Christians in the vital sense, and that to leave them free would therefore
accomplish nothing at all. To rely on the Church, however, as a method of
defeating the human determination to pervert the Gospel, was to rely on
the means of perversion which men had most frequently used. Harnack
thought that Christianity could be saved by men who had set themselves
free from ecclesiasticism; Kierkegaard would have unhesitatingly identified
Bismarckian Protestantism as the same well-fed avoidance of the religious
problem which he had marked down in Denmark fifty years before. He
would probably also have called in evidence the *Kulturkampf*, the synthetic
conflict which Bismarck generated between the new German Empire and
the Catholic Church in Germany (1870–78).

This comparison may be supplemented by a brief discussion of two other
theological writers whose work casts light on Kierkegaard's position. The
first was Anton de Lagarde (1827–91), who was German despite the name
which he took in 1854. A weather-beaten signpost to wrong roads that were
followed later, the German historian, Golo Mann, called him. Lagarde's
outlook was permanently affected by the abortive German revolutions of
1848. He incarnated all too perfectly the nationalist revulsion against any
radical changes in the structure of society. He wanted to purge Christianity
of all traces of Judaism, in order to replace it with a truly German religion
in which the soul of the nation would find expression. Thus he was one of
the fore-runners of the willingly anti-semitic German-Christian Church
which briefly served Hitler's purposes in the 1930s. For Lagarde, suffering
from the same social climate as Kierkegaard, the conclusion was not
individualism but a frightened totalitarianism which merged the Church
into the nation-state, and invented a new, more hysterical kind of revivalism, for which Jewishness became the presence of the Devil, and salvation
a superficial loss of identity in the oneness of the group, not in the least
like the profound destruction of the self relentlessly pursued by a serious
student of renunciation like Simone Weil.

'The nation is an organism', Lagarde said, 'and must have a soul. This
soul must have a unity. It is surely a misfortune if Germany remains
divided in two or more parts. Germany does not want a Catholicism minus

[1] *ib.* p. 275.

the Pope, nor a Protestantism minus a greater or smaller number of dogmas, but a new life which would put the old life to death.' He used Judaism as the symbol of everything that he hated, the materialism of the post-1870 Empire, for example. 'The Jews, as their prophets have often said, are a stiff-necked people . . . But the Gospel seeks salvation not in the will, but in the breaking of the will, in the Cross, which the Jew rejects as foolishness. Only when each nation crucifies the will of the Jew will the Jew be redeemed from himself, and in that way, and only in that way shall we be saved from the Jew.' Lagarde's reputation in middle-class German Protestantism was too great for one simply to dismiss this as unrepresentative or insane.

It may seem unkind to compare Lagarde's destructive religious national-ism with F. D. Maurice's eagerness to reinforce the idea of the 'nation' with the mystical offices of the 'Church'. Maurice was, of course, untouched by anti-semitism and the worst that his enthusiasm for the 'national Church' may be said to have legitimized was a handful of imperialist episcopal speeches at the time of the South African War (1899–1902). Maurice, nevertheless, was reacting to the same cultural pressures as were affecting Lagarde, and this British blend of Church and state fell on the same side of the line as the German's headier theology. Like Lagarde, Maurice was deeply affected by the social division of industrialized society; he feared the onset of a radically pluralistic culture. He expressed his reaction in theo-logical terms by saying that the Church was the servant of the divine order which God willed for men, and must therefore seek to reconcile the hostile classes to one another; to foster the emergence of social harmony was essentially the task of the National Church. Maurice had a Burkean sense of social and political continuity, and this has often won him the sympathy of later conservative-minded theologians. For him the union between Church and state in England was hallowed by time and providence, an object of veneration Even as late as 1870 he still believed that the clergy of the Church of England possessed the secret of 'nation-forming', a process of spiritual education which was denied to both the state and Nonconformity. He could not tolerate any suggestion of ecclesiastical discontinuity, though he did not share Newman's enthusiasm for episcopal succession as the specific symbol of the unity of the past; his defence of church establishment was as absolute as Kierkegaard's criticism of it.

Kierkegaard's individualism about the Church has therefore to be understood against the background of these other attitudes, this Victorian romanticism about the historical Church on the one hand, and Lagarde's much more vicious and political version of the organic doctrine on the other. There was never any question in the Victorian period of the doctrine of the Church either being neglected or of shrinking to a mere religious individualism: Kierkegaard's existentialist approach, which had little impact before 1900, contrasted strongly with the corporate theologies of the Church which dominated both Catholicism and Protestantism. It was in the twentieth century, and as often as not in the books of biblical critics, that the most extreme rejection of the idea of the Church was to be found. Summarizing the position in *Jesus and His Church* (1938) R. N. Flew said that the statement that 'Jesus founded no Church' had become almost a dogma of critical orthodoxy: E. F. Scott had declared that Jesus 'had not consciously formed a society', though the historical Church was 'the inevitable outcome of his work'; Troeltsch assumed that the first outstanding characteristic of the ethics of Jesus was an unlimited, unqualified individualism, and then asserted that during the lifetime of Jesus there was no sign of an organized community.[1] Such writers did not want to abolish the Church but regarded it as formed historically by the voluntary association of baptized or converted people; they thought that the institutionalization of the sacraments was a human, not a divine decision. In the light of the gradually changing religious crisis which has been described in these pages this was not surprising; there had been moments in modern Christian history when the survival of the possibility of belief had seemed much more important than the status of membership of the Church.

After 1918, however, the context of the doctrine changed as the ecumenical movement grew. Many causes (see, for example, B. Wilson, *Religion in a Secular Society*, 1966) combined to foster its growth. Historically, however, the breach between the traditional Churches and the modern state, and the further separation between the older religious culture and a newer, much less religious one, had thrown the Church as a whole back on itself, while on the mission-fields away from Europe and North America this feeling of isolation was reinforced by the increasing resistance of non-Christian religious cultures. There was no longer any question, as had been assumed in the over-confident early nineteenth-century missiology, of the rapid disintegration of the outworn Buddhist, Hindu or Islamic interpretations of existence. Unity began to seem a socially and politically desirable religious goal in the west. Theologians returned to the discussion of the nature of the Church and of the Church's unity, trying to do two separate things:

(a) to find new, or more convincingly stated, grounds for asserting the supernatural nature of the Church over against the aggressive surrounding societies (a repetition of the psychological pressures which had produced Tractarianism in the 1830s purely in terms of the collapse of the *ancien régime*);

(b) to find new or more convincing grounds for affirming the priority of visible ecclesiastical unity as such, as against, for example, the Harnackian position (see above) that institutional plurality, or variety, was of the essence of true Christianity.

The ecumenical movement produced no major writing, but an orthodoxy emerged that based itself on a fresh appeal to the evidence about the Church to be found in the Bible, here often treated as though the historical-critical method somehow did not apply. The primary point was that the Church should not be thought of as secondary to the Gospel. 'Any such conception of the relation between Gospel and Church is not true to the Bible, where Israel is constituted the People of God by faith. Throughout the New Testament justification by faith has corporate no less than individual reference. By faith in Christ a man becomes a member of the body. In the New Testament, moreover, this is wholly consistent with the

[1] R. N. Flew, *Jesus and His Church* (1938), pp. 24–5.

recognition of the individual and his personal encounter and communion with God in Christ . . . The privileges of the Gospel involve the believer in duties (worship, service) many of which can only be performed corporately.'

It was therefore possible to argue that 'God in Christ by the Spirit takes the initiative in bringing into being a people which is his Church; in entrusting it, though not as its own property, with means of grace . . . Such a community must have an order, not merely in the sense of disciplinary rules, such as any voluntary society needs, but as structure, so as to be itself and perform its proper functions. The essential structure of the Church is divinely determined, since it is Christ's Church, not ours. For this, as for Christian faith in general, we look to the Bible to discover "the given", i.e. what God has appointed.'

And so the very explicit conclusion might be reached that 'what is given in Order includes worship, word, sacraments, ministry, pastoral care, discipline of members, and participation of members in regulating the common life. These are gifts of the one Spirit and should operate harmoniously. It is true that the New Testament provides no fixed and self-evident pattern in which all these cohere, but some of the given elements help to shape other elements in Order. For example, the sacrament of Holy Communion involves the saying of certain words and the performing of certain actions, and requires rules as to who shall say and perform them and who shall be admitted to it.'

These passages on organic unity come from the 1963 *Report* of the Conversations between the Church of England and the Methodist Church (pp. 20–21) and they typify the ecclesiology of a generation. God brought those whom he saved into a single community (which men had wrongly divided), which had an essential (not arbitrary or widely variable) structure which was not only divinely determined but scripturally revealed, so that ministry, pastoral care and discipline of members were gifts of the one Spirit, for example. And this Report went on to say that although it might not be possible to prove from first principles that Church Order required a separated, specialized ministry, 'the real reason for having it is that the ministry is "given" in the New Testament, i.e. it both exists and is described as given by God' (p. 22). The ecclesiology of the period constantly assumed the need for a single, world-wide set of visible, ecclesiastical institutions, hierarchically organized on the basis of the 'historic episcopate', though it was significant of a deeper level of disagreement that the British Methodist representatives who accepted these premises in practice added that of course the Methodist Conference did not claim that either episcopacy or any form of organization even in the Apostolic Church should be determinative for the Church for all time.

This ecclesiology became more important after the Second Vatican Council (1964) under the inspiration of Pope John XXIII had made moves which suggested that the monarchical interpretation of the Papal office, which had been especially dominant since the Council of 1870, might now be modified. The documents of the Council called the Pope 'the pastor of the whole Church', rather than, more traditionally, 'the head of the Church'; the papal primacy was described as arising from the idea and existence of

the Church, rather than the Church being described as deriving its being
from the primacy. The position of the Roman Catholic episcopate in
relation to the Pope was strengthened when the Council laid down that
bishops received their full authority from their consecration and not from
their appointment by the Pope; this was an old issue which the Council of
1870 had left unsettled but which as recent a Pope as Pius XII had tried
to determine in favour of papal authority in his encyclical *Mystici Corporis
Christi* (1943). Not only was it now held that the primacy was a ministry
of service rather than a dominion or source of power, but some effort was
made to set up institutions to embody the idea that the Pope and his
bishops shared a collegial responsibility for the government of the whole
Church. The pressure of Roman history was obvious in all this; the Council
must have seemed at times thronged by silent, shadowy witnesses; every
word that was spoken had multiple references in the past. Nothing that
happened was decisively liberal and Paul VI did not maintain the Johannine momentum of the Council, but the ecumenical possibility remained
that an episcopally united majority of Protestantism might in the not too
distant future come to terms with a Catholicism less papal, less curial and
less clerical.[1]

Theologically, the post-1918 approach assumed that the idea of the
Church as a supernatural as well as a historical body could be found in the
New Testament and that the structure of the Church – institutions essential
to its existence – was also divinely revealed in the Scriptures. Moreover, the
Church thus revealed could be recognized in history; what was divinely
given could be historically identified. Driven from the cultural centre of
modern western civilization the Church must unite in order to re-evangelize
what was in danger of becoming a lost planet.

Thus one side of nineteenth-century ecclesiology – that which emphasized
the unity, sanctity and necessity of the visible, hierarchical Church to
which every Christian must belong – had largely triumphed. The triumph
had come late, however. There was less theological satisfaction with their
general doctrine than the new ecumenical school admitted. At the moment
when ecclesiological unanimity seemed to have dawned theology swung off
into a more critical position. At the first Assembly of the World Council of
Churches (1948), for example, Karl Barth, without invoking the historical-
critical attitude to the Bible, questioned the view that the Church possessed
a divinely given structure continuously visible in history especially in terms
of creeds, ministry and sacraments; for Barth, the Church was to be thought
of as occurring in history as a discontinuous series of faith-events. A similar
line was taken by Rudolf Bultmann, for whom it was only in a paradoxical
sense that the Church was identical with ecclesiastical institutions which
might be observed as sociological phenomena in secular history; the true
Church was an eschatological phenomenon which might possess a con-
gregational visibility but was nevertheless a part of the age to come,

---

[1] See *Authority in the Church*, a statement agreed by the Anglican-Roman Catholic
International Commission (1977), especially p. 18, where the Commission seemed to
envisage that in any future union the see of Rome should hold a modified universal
primacy.

secularly *in*visible, but to be grasped by the eye of faith. Bultmann always expounded his understanding of the Church in the context of the saving event, so that the Church's transcendent life in Christ might not be concealed by its visible institutions, such as the ministry.

At first sight what was happening was a recrudescence of the old antithesis between institutionalized religion and what the late nineteenth-century French anti-dogmatic liberal theologian, André Sabatier, called the 'religion of the Spirit'. This was certainly Emil Brunner's thesis in *The Misunderstanding of the Church* (1953), a kind of exaggerated version of Harnack's *Essence of Christianity* (1900), in which Brunner (himself a contemporary of Barth and Bultmann) said that the Church of the New Testament period was a spirit-filled community which vanished as soon as it institutionalized itself; the true Church could not be given institutional form, and so what was institutionalized was not the true Church. Brunner did not want to abolish the existing Church, however. For him, as for Karl Barth, the model of the ideal Church was really a small local organism living in as close a relation as possible to the age to come. In the Protestant past, this model had been used by very diverse groups, the Puritan Independents, for example, and by F. D. Maurice and the early Christian Socialists.

There was a Roman Catholic parallel to this movement of ideas, in such books as *Do We Need the Church?* (1969) by Richard McBrien, and Hans Küng's *The Church* (1967). Küng, like the Protestant ecumenical theologians, appealed to the New Testament as his authority for the doctrine of the Church. His conclusion, however, was less conventional. Describing what he took to be the meaning of the Pauline evidence, he said that (a) there appeared to be no monarchical episcopate in the Pauline communities at all; (b) there was no uncontrovertible evidence that the office of presbyter existed in these communities; (c) that the Pauline letters contained no clear evidence of ordination.

Paul, Küng said, would not have regarded his church-order as provisional. It was all the more important, therefore, that in the type-case of Corinth 'the burden of proof lies with those who wish to assert that there existed in the Corinthian community in Paul's time an office of leadership, whether elders or the later kind of monarchical episcopate', (p. 403). In Küng's opinion the elder-episcopate developed separately on a Palestinian basis. Neither system could claim to be original. (There was not, in other words, according to the Catholic exegete, the divinely-given structure, accessible in both the New Testament and in later history, to which the Anglican-Methodist documents of the 1960s, for instance, had appealed). And so Küng used language very similar to Emil Brunner's: 'a frightening gulf separates the Church of today from the constitution of the original Church' (p. 413).

Küng said that traditional ecclesiology had turned to history and tradition in general to defend its arbitrary conclusions, ignoring or minimizing the extent to which the earliest New Testament data failed to confirm what was asserted. He wanted to avoid what he called the Protestant tactic of taking sides, specifically of taking an anti-institutional side. In

the light of the Pauline evidence as he interpreted it, however, he underlined the difficulty of justifying 'any special commission to the ministry by
men, given that each man has received his charism, his vocation, directly
from God. Is the inner impulse not sufficient?' (p. 422).

As Küng said, one could solve the problem by arguing that as a matter
of fact the bureaucratization of charisms was the natural course of the
historical development of any religion, but this solution left the Christian
ministry only one more example of 'ministry' in general. One could also
appeal to the need for order (and this reminds one of the Anglican-Methodist
Report of 1963 which specifically claimed that order was not contrary to the
gospel; its function was to express the gospel and to contribute to its
fulfilment in life). Küng was not impressed by this argument, because the
alleged chaos of the cults did not strike him as necessarily worse than the
sterility which could be imposed by the systematization of ministry.
Pastors had done as much harm as prophets, he said (which was not the
usual opinion of the ecumenical theologians), and the statement was really
a significant concession to historical evidence in a subject (ecclesiology)
which had never taken kindly to inconvenient data. The pastoral quest for
power, Küng said, dissolved the original unity of West and East. In
balancing arguments like this he was keeping faith with his original premise
that neither the Pauline nor the Palestinian church-type represented the
form of the true Church which had subsequently been corrupted. Küng
might not want to contradict the statement that 'the essential structure of
the Church is divinely determined', if only because the alternative was so
far-reaching in its effects, but he showed no confidence that such a structure
could be deduced from the contents of the New Testament.

Küng's own solution of the problem – to describe the Pauline communities as having an interim, eschatological structure – was unsatisfactory, all
the more so because he wished to reform the Roman Church in the direction
of the Pauline rather than the Palestinian position. Nor could he find a
secure New Testament basis for the papal primacy, which he redefined as
a primacy of service which could be attained 'through the voluntary
renunciation of the power which has in practice become associated with the
Petrine ministry, through a long and problematical historical development,
and has partly helped it and also seriously injured it' (p. 472).

In Küng's work, radical in its Catholic context, one sees another example
of the working-out of the historical-critical method in the field of ecclesiology. His use of the biblical material was not as definitive as he supposed,
however. Like most Protestant ecumenical scholars, he could not rid himself of the belief that there must exist somewhere an authoritative way of
using the New Testament data, that one must be able to arrive at an unambiguous conclusion which would serve as an absolute basis for decision
today. In reality, the vital point about the New Testament data about the
Church was their ambiguity, their Pauline-Palestinian content (as Küng
himself put it). The history of the Church, as well as the history of the
doctrine of the Church, has oscillated between these models of the perfect
community; but history does not justify the assumption that a single,
essential and definable structure was nevertheless divinely and clearly

revealed in the Scriptures. Unity was a relative term, more and less useful in different historical contexts.

The question of historical context was becoming as important as the question of what the New Testament said, and some of the darker sayings in *Letters and Papers from Prison* (E.T. 1953), by Dietrich Bonhoeffer (1909–45), seemed to imply that the church-types of the past, whether Pauline or Palestinian, had lost their relevance because they were based on cultural assumptions which no longer held good. If the European way of life had become secularized, one could only speak of God by using the secular as a mode of the transcendent, and this applied as much to the forms of the Church as to the language of theology. If a time was coming when men could no longer be religious at all, then Christianity itself would have to become 'religionless' as well. Bonhoeffer's theology was orthodox enough; what had changed for him was the world outside the Church. His cruel experience had driven him beyond Matthew Arnold's conclusion: now men *could* do without Christianity, human nature had changed, there was no religious *a priori*, and therefore one did not really know how to alter the form of the Church. Thirty years later the disappearance of religion no longer seemed as inevitable, because even alienation could be historicized, and so ceased to threaten a permanent condition; but it was still not clear how the form of the Church should be changed.

Bonhoeffer's prison writings pointed towards a new development of the doctrine of the Church to which he did not survive to contribute. The ecumenical theologians had concentrated on the problem of unity and therefore on problems of church-structure. Karl Barth and Rudolf Bult-mann had restated the characteristic Protestant criticism that personal faith must take precedence over structure, that faith was more often in danger from organization than organization from personal faith. Hans Küng had given theological expression to the new demand for ecclesiastical reform which swept through the Roman Catholic Church at the time of the second Vatican Council, and which produced, for example, a long agitation for the abandonment of sacerdotal celibacy. All these theologians, however, took for granted the survival of the ecclesia in unbroken visible continuity with the traditions of the past; they perpetuated the Mauricean belief that nothing was worse than a breach of continuity, that Burke (to put it in English terms) was your only political theologian of the Church. Some of Bonhoeffer's successors suspected, however, that the cultural revolution (of which Kierkegaard had already foreseen the probable result) was reaching a climax in which a fundamental social discontinuity was beginning to take shape. This meant that the gravest weakness of the twentieth-century western Church was its deep sociological involvement as a set of historical institutions in precisely the cultural order that was passing away. A passion for continuity might now be no more than a death-wish. It was true that the Church as an institution had survived the collapse of the Roman world and had even to some extent determined the form of the medieval culture which had followed it, but the history of Europe between 1500 and 1914 did not prove that the Church had adapted itself significantly to change. Now in the twentieth century a new situation was crystallizing in which a hierarchical ecclesia which laid claim to absolute powers of discipline and dogmatic definition no longer seemed particularly appropriate. The concept of a 'divinely-given structure', which had had a long run since its revival in the 1830s, was beginning to fall into the background theologically. This did not entail the substitution of a third church-type for both the Pauline and Palestinian forms; nor did it mean that the idea of ecclesiastical institutions was called permanently in doubt; rather, there was a growing feeling that new forms of the ecclesia must be allowed to manifest themselves as society transformed itself; that, instead of trying to deduce the structure of the Church from some form of the doctrine of the Church, one must allow the doctrine of the Church to reflect the life of the actual Christian community as it finds itself moving from one new historical situation to another.

There remains one deep area of disagreement between orthodox and liberal theologians. Liberals cannot really accept the view that the Church as a visible institution has a special competence to proclaim and safeguard the gospel, and therefore must have effective means to do so. Orthodox theologians, on the other hand, while granting that such institutions have not always acted correctly, believe in the indefectibility of the Church, which Christ will never desert and which the Holy Spirit will lead into all truth. When the Anglican-Roman Catholic International Commission reported on 'Authority in the Church' in 1976 it could still maintain that when the Church met in ecumenical council its decisions on fundamental matters of faith excluded what was erroneous because, being faithful to Scripture and consistent with Tradition, they were protected from error by the Holy Spirit.[1] The strict liberal view might be that liberation from error was not so easily obtained, and that truth had to be possessed in faith, not in such relative certainty.

---

[1] *ib.* pp. 16–17. The Report was dated Venice, 1976, and published 1977.

IV

SOCIAL THEOLOGY IN THE WHOLE PERIOD

Social theology began to change rapidly in the nineteenth century. This was because the ongoing industrial revolution, and the social revolution which was bound up with it – both of which must be taken for granted here – changed the data with which the theologian had to work and compelled him, in some cases at any rate, to re-examine his assumptions about the social teaching of the Bible. Over a short period of time western society moved from conditions of comparative poverty, insecurity and dependence upon nature to comparative wealth, security and freedom of choice; the hierarchy of the *ancien régime* became the class structure of Victorian society; secular political assumptions and goals altered.

These social changes, and the intellectual activity they generated, affected theologians all the more profoundly because by the mid-eighteenth century they had come very much to terms with the *ancien régime*. Roman Catholic theology, for example, had committed itself so deeply to the idea that monarchy was the proper form of Christian government that it was not until the late nineteenth century that Leo XIII, realizing that the restoration of the French monarchy in any form had now become extremely unlikely, officially granted the possibility of a divine republic; in *Diuturnum Illud* (1881) he said that popular democracy could be reconciled with the traditional doctrine as to the right origin of political power, because the electors only chose the holders of authority and were not the source of the authority itself.

Protestantism, though not as devoted as Roman Catholicism to the monarchical principle, had certainly reconciled itself to the established order by about 1750. In its earlier, more extreme period, Protestant sectarianism had encouraged a politics of withdrawal from society. The remnant of the saints no longer hoped to change the world as a political reality but moved out into the wilderness to offer God perfect service, as in the case of the Puritans who sailed to America in the seventeenth century; there could be a similar kind of withdrawal in Roman Catholicism, as when the late-seventeenth-century Jansenists opted out of politics in despair at the apparent invincibility of French absolutism. In the Protestant world the fires of apocalyptic imagery had burnt low and the new energy of eighteenth-century evangelicalism ran into pietist movements like British Methodism whose leader, John Wesley, summed up his attitude to political authority in words which were not so very different from those which a contemporary Roman Catholic might have used:

'The supposition, then, that the people are the origin of power is every way indefensible. It is absolutely overturned by the very principle on which it is supposed to stand; namely, that a right of choosing governors belongs to every partaker of human nature. If this be so, then it belongs to every individual of the human species; consequently, not to freeholders only, but to all men; not to men only, but to women also; nor only to adult men and women, to those who have lived one and twenty years, but to those who have lived eighteen or twenty; as well as those who have lived threescore. But none ever did maintain this, nor probably ever will. Therefore this boasted principle falls to the ground, and the whole superstructure with it. So common sense brings us back to the grand truth, "There is no power but of God".'[1] The conclusion of the argument comes, of course, from St. Paul's Epistle to the Romans. The common sense which Wesley was defending was the common sense of revelation as he interpreted it, leading, in his own case, to passionate support for George III against the American revolutionaries.

The opposite, more radical tradition did not die out altogether. One can trace a line from the seventeenth-century republican propagandist, James Harrington (1611–77), through Moses Lowman, a presbyterian whose *Dissertation on the Civil Government of the Hebrews* was published in 1740, to the young and temporarily radical S. T. Coleridge, who stated in his 'Lectures on Revealed Religion', delivered in Bristol in 1795 but not published in his lifetime, that 'Jesus Christ forbids to his disciples all property and teaches us that accumulation was incompatible with their salvation'. Coleridge did not actually advocate equality of possessions, but rather the having all things in common, adding, however, that 'this part of Christian doctrine, which indeed is almost the whole of it, soon was corrupted'. The same lectures contained a sharp rejection of commerce and urban life:

'The smoakes that rise from our crowded Townes hide from us the face of Heaven. In the country, the Love and Power of the great Invisible are everywhere perspicuous, and by degrees we become partakers of that which we are accustomed to contemplate. The beautiful and the Good are miniatures on the Heart of the contemplater as the surrounding landscape on a convex mirror. But in Cities God is everywhere removed from our sight and Man obtruded upon us – not Man, the work of God, but the debased offspring of Luxury and Want.'[2]

It is interesting that the young Coleridge reasserted the world-renouncing themes of primitive Christianity just when the pace of industrial change was quickening. That Christianity, properly defined, could not come to terms with the economic expansion of the west was frequently to be maintained in the course of the nineteenth century, sometimes in unexpected quarters, as in the writings of Nietzsche or Franz Overbeck (1837–1905). Coleridge, of course, abandoned his youthful radicalism, and did not develop the deeper questions about the nature of Christianity which this ascetic, world-renouncing interpretation of its early history implied; in his later years as an apologist for the Church of England he was to emphasize the

[1] J. Wesley, 'Thoughts Concerning the Origin of Power', in *Works*, vol. 11 (1865), p. 50.
[2] S. T. Coleridge, *Works*, ed. L. Patton and P. Mann, vol. 1 (1971), p. 226.

oneness of a society from which it was inconceivable that Christians should want to withdraw at all.

The handful of Christian radicals apart, most eighteenth-century theologians accepted the permanence of a static, divinely ordained society on a hierarchical pattern, in which Church and State were closely united – a community in which, historically speaking, change had generally occurred too slowly in the past to become an issue in itself. Eighteenth-century German Lutheranism offers an example of the way in which the critical, liberal rationalism of the Enlightenment had only a limited effect on Christian social thought. In the German Lutheran Churches the change to a more rationalist outlook took place in the 1760s. Until then preaching had remained for the most part either orthodox – concerned with the faithful as part of the Lutheran Confession, which had to be clearly distinguished from the Calvinist Reformed as well as the Roman Church; or pietist – concerned more with the subjective side of the religious life, and with man as needing to be saved and needing to bear witness to salvation. Then the change came. The Lutheran preachers of the Enlightenment wanted to end what for them had become a tiresome battle over obscure and trivial theological distinctions; they also rejected the orthodox description of this life as a vale of tears. The preaching of morality (instead of doctrine) began as an escape from the past, not only into a more tolerant atmosphere but also into a life which actually seemed more religious, because more committed to sincere behaviour than to formal belief.

This new Lutheranism did not look forward to any new order of society. Even the most rationalist of the later eighteenth-century Lutheran preachers advised domestic servants, for example, that their duty and happiness lay in making their masters free and happy. 'Masters will always be masters and servants will always be servants', wrote C. F. Sintenis (1750–1820). For the most part the Lutheran preachers supported the existing regime of German princely states, though Sintenis sometimes spoke of the possibility of the prince's advisers having been elected by the people. The ideal prince would himself be 'enlightened'; he would identify with the bourgeoisie instead of with the aristocracy; he would promote men on account of merit instead of birth; he would keep out of war and seek to improve his country's economic position. The most that these theologians wanted politically was a gentle modification of the *ancien régime* in favour of the bourgeoisie and at the expense of the landed class; they neither foresaw nor wanted revolution. They had transformed the sixteenth-century idea of 'vocation' or 'calling', fundamental to Martin Luther's own view of society, into a doctrine of social obedience, which was used to persuade the lower orders to content themselves with their limited existence.

At the end of the eighteenth century, therefore, Christian opinion still largely supported the traditional idea of a hierarchical society ordained by God and incapable of major useful change; some theologians, however, like the Lutherans referred to above, reflected the demands of the bourgeoisie for greater intellectual freedom and economic power. (Among the theological offshoots of this campaign for intellectual liberty was the secularist movement, which in England was rooted in the writings of Tom Paine, from whom the tradition passed to Carlile (1790–1843), the more compromising Holyoake (1817–1906) who was willing to work with groups like the Christian Socialists, and Charles Bradlaugh (1833–91), who presided over the last aggressive phase between 1860 and 1900.) The most radical political thinkers of the early nineteenth century, Saint-Simon (1760–1825), Robert Owen (1771–1858) and Charles Fourier (1772–1837), rejected orthodox Christianity together with the existing social system, though Saint-Simon, like Rousseau, invented his own religious system because he did not believe that human society could function successfully without one.

What the utopian schemes of this group of socialist thinkers underlines was that the collapse of Christendom was leaving western society without any generally accepted sanction or source of common authority in economic affairs. As Emile Durkheim wrote in his study of the Saint-Simonians: 'What is needed if social order is to reign is that the mass of men be content with their lot. But what is needed for them to be content is not that they have more or less, but that they be convinced that they have no right to more.' (Which was the social outcome of hierarchical societies in general.) 'And for this it is absolutely essential that there be an authority whose superiority they acknowledge and which tells them what is right. For an individual committed only to the pressure of his needs will never admit that he has reached the extreme limit of his rightful portion. If he is not conscious of a force above him which he respects, which stops him and tells him with authority that the compensation due to him is fulfilled, then inevitably he will expect as due to him all that his needs demand . . . For it to be otherwise, a moral power is required whose superiority he recognizes and which cries out "You must go no further". This was precisely the rôle played in the older society by the (religious) powers whose progressive dethronement Saint-Simon notes. Religion instructed the humble to be content with their situation at the same time as it taught them that the social order is providential, that it is God himself who has determined everyone's share; and giving them glimpses beyond this earth of another world where everything will be balanced, it stopped them from feeling aggrieved.'[1]

This decline of the religious sanction on human economic expectation coincided with the rapid growth of industry and technology. One consequence, especially in the more developed industrial countries, was the gradual replacement of the older hierarchical structure by a new kind of class structure to which Christian theology was bound to take time to adjust itself. It was natural for some theologians to interpret this new pattern of classes as only the former hierarchy in a modern dress, to fix the stamp of the divine approval on Capital and Labour, for example, and to assume that correct Christian political solutions would always be found by creating harmony between the two. A God of Love must be served through social co-operation, not through social conflict, it was assumed, and the idea of co-operation was seen as excluding the possibility of basic changes in the given social structure. One can exaggerate the extent to

[1] E. Durkheim, *Socialism* (New York, 1967), pp. 242–43.

which the underprivileged had ever willingly borne the deprivations which
the European social system had inflicted upon them; in any case, after 1815
the class structure itself became a vehicle of working-class demands for
change. Theologians who argued that Capital must always be Capital and
Labour must always be Labour were not well-placed to satisfy these
demands theologically.

Variations on this theme dominated much of the social theology of the
nineteenth century. After 1815, as after most periods of intense, prolonged
warfare, there was a widespread desire in the wealthier classes for a return
to a golden age of international peace, social stability and religious certainty.
Theologians, both Roman Catholic (de Maistre, for example), and Protestant
(Coleridge), reaffirmed the very unity of society and Christianity which the
eighteenth-century philosophes had ridiculed and the revolutionaries had
done their best to abolish. By 1848, however, it was clear that such a unity
would have to be restored, not preserved, and it was the importance of the
Christian Socialism advocated by J. M. Ludlow in 1848 that he asserted
that one could no longer defend the existing social and economic system as
ordained by God. In 1849, after the terrible fighting between the French
workers and the middle classes in Paris, Ludlow said:

> In the name of a God of love let us not lose the warning. Capital and
> Labour cannot thus be suffered to remain at issue with one another.
> They must be harmonized, they must be associated. It is not a
> machinery that will do this, without God's grace shed abroad in our
> hearts; but can it be done without a change in machinery? Is it
> Christian, is it human, to leave labour – that is, the nerves, the muscles
> and lifeblood of our fellow-creatures – to the scientific operation of
> the 'laws of supply and demand'? to deem oneself justified in paying
> the 'current rate of wages' when that current rate of wages is not
> sufficient to support life? Look to the four days slaughter in Paris;
> see whether they are not the logical result of the competitive, the
> selfish system.[1]

Ludlow published this in *Politics for the People*, the weekly paper which
the Anglican Christian Socialists (Ludlow, Charles Kingsley, F. D. Maurice)
issued in 1848–49. They were entitled to call themselves 'Christian Socialists'
because to some extent they believed that the social problems of the time
could not be solved by a change of attitudes alone, by that mysterious warm-
ing of the heart on which many religious writers relied to bring about social
transformation – as though Charles Dickens's *Christmas Carol* offered a
serious image of the way in which men were moved to reform their behaviour
and their society. A reversal of the trend towards unlimited individualism
must, they thought, be embodied in visible economic institutions, the
industrial co-operative, for instance, and trade unions inspired by a radical
Christian understanding of the proper forms of social advancement for their
members. Maurice, it is true, easily fell back on the language of feeling,
exhorting both Capital and Labour to look 'not for differences but agreement, seeking to reconcile divisions and not to make them'; then everybody

[1] *Politics for the People*, p. 197.

would understand and feel 'what a blessing and privilege it is to be a member of the Great English Partnership'.[1] All the Christian Socialists agreed that a merely secular socialism could not reunite society into a harmonious co-operative enterprise. Charles Kingsley said that 'men will never be joined in true brotherhood by mere plans to give them a self-interest in common, as the Socialists have tried to do. No, to feel for each other they must first feel with each other. To have their sympathies in common, they must have, not an object of gain, but an object of admiration in common; to know that they are brothers, they must feel that they have One Father.'[2]

Kingsley, Ludlow and Maurice were reacting against the secularization of politics which had set in since the late eighteenth century and which produced its most famous document, *The Communist Manifesto*, in 1848, the same year which witnessed the appearance of the short-lived *Politics for the People*. The Christian Socialists wanted to capture the revolutionary socialist tradition for Christianity, and Ludlow dreamed briefly of introducing a new economic system of industrial organization through the formation of producer as well as distributor co-operatives: once these associations had expanded on a national scale (for he did not think in terms of revolution) they would be able to decide on wages and prices nationally and for the public good. Ludlow believed in what he called 'Collective Mastership' in a self-governing community. 'So long as each labours for all as all labour for him', he wrote, 'and endeavours always to do his best, because he knows that he will receive the best that can be given him, Communism, pure Communism, will, I feel sure, exhibit the very type of a flourishing society.'[3] This new society was the highest earthly embodiment of the Christian Church. For Ludlow, in the first flush of the Christian Socialist movement at any rate, the gospel of Christ was wholly incompatible with a political economy which proclaimed self-interest to be the pivot of social action, or with a system of trade based wholly on the incentive of private profit. A theologically true society could be created only by faith in Christ working through a true Church, but, Ludlow admitted in 1850:

> I feel more and more that it is utterly impossible to make Christian Socialism what it ought to be, a true Church-movement among the people, unless we can Americanise the Church by giving her true self-government in convocation . . . it seems quite clear to me that, with what I have called an Americanised Church we could fairly conquer the working-classes of this country, that is to say, the very heart of English society, for Christ, and that if we do not, nobody else will, and that we never shall, without sweeping church-reform.[4]

Such ideas only alarmed Maurice, who rejected democracy on his own biblical grounds and who dismissed all schemes for human organization

[1] *ib.* p. 274.
[2] *ib.* p. 185.
[3] *The Christian Socialist*, vol. 1, p. 234.
[4] T. Christensen, *Origin and History of Christian Socialism* (1962), p. 161.

beyond the parish level as 'the organisation of evil powers for the sake of producing good effects'. Maurice, who resembled Coleridge, the political conservative, much more than Ludlow ever did, was fundamentally a symbolist, not a technologist. The Divine Order, which rested on fellowship and co-operation, already existed; God himself constantly renewed men's willingness to live in brotherhood. The value of the idea of association to Maurice was simply as a way of proclaiming this already given divine order, but he explicitly denied in the first of the *Tracts on Christian Socialism* that he wanted to create 'a great combination for the reorganising all the trades of the cities and the agriculture of the country'. As he saw it, there could not be a more divine order than what was already given, because any new social system would be exposed to the same strains from the selfishness, ignorance and competitiveness of man. His view of society was largely psychological: he did not separate an industrial system, which might be more or less 'christian', from the individual people, capitalists as well as workers, who made up the industrial structure which he knew. Maurice's habit of seeking to limit Christian action to the proclamation of truth on a parochial scale suggests that he was more of an evangelical pietist than he consciously admitted. Ludlow's failure to convert his leader to the need for nationally organised action symbolized his wider failure to democratize the Church of England or to persuade the majority of its members to accept as their personal social ideal the model of society which he advocated. One must not exaggerate the significance of his failure. There was never any chance of success. Maurice finally abandoned the Christian Socialist movement in 1854 for the more congenial field of the London Working Men's College. It remains true that after 1860 religious bodies had little influence on the development of the Labour Movement in England – as elsewhere, the revolutionary tradition absorbed Marx, not Christian Socialism.

Ludlow's case was not altogether dissimilar from that of Lamennais (1782–1854), the ablest of the nineteenth-century French liberal Catholics. Once he had been forced to give up, by 1834, the hope that the Papacy could be persuaded to preside over the democratization of the Roman Catholic Church, Lamennais ceased to believe that ecclesiastical institutions could be used to transform society as a whole. Interpreting the struggle of the people for political power as a mystical projection of the will of God, he substituted faith in a revolutionary people for faith in a revolutionary Church. This was a step which Ludlow was not able to take; he could not identify himself totally with the working-classes unless the working-classes first identified themselves with the Church of England, a position made all the more desperate by the fact that, like Lamennais, he had a low opinion of the Anglican Church as he found it. Lamennais was less politically inhibited. No one, he said, was born into the world with a right to command others; therefore, there should be no intermediary between God and the people. 'I am a disciple of Christ, not of the Church', he said, a remark which rejected the value of a hierarchical society. Both Ludlow and Marx (but not Coleridge or Maurice) wanted to change the economic structure of society, Ludlow in order to enable men to express the communal core of the Gospel through their social institutions, Marx – religiously speaking – in

order to make men realize that they did not depend on God at all, and that
they did not need to project him. Lamennais' interests remained more
strictly political – he believed that the people would express the will of God
if they were given the opportunity through a democratic system based on
universal suffrage. If one compares F. D. Maurice, Ludlow and Lamennais
in terms of their attitude to the decisive social fact of the nineteenth
century, the change from a static to a dynamic economic system in the
west, one finds that Maurice, apart from a brief period when he was
influenced by Ludlow, attached little importance to the forms of society or
to the likelihood of being able to change them, but constantly asked men to
look through the superficial structure of society to the divine order which
always underlay it; that Ludlow, while temperamentally opposed to this
platonic conservatism, and convinced that the Gospel required a new
socio-economic form – 'there must be a Socialist politics and a Socialist
medicine, Socialist literature and Socialist art, Socialist science and Socialist
law, as well as Socialist trade and industry' – believed that such social
changes must be inspired by a religious rather than a political movement,
but despaired once he realized that Maurice was not the man to lead one;
while Lamennais, politically much the most sophisticated of the three, the
clearest in his conviction that the religious forces of Europe could not
indefinitely deny, though they might indefinitely lament, the passing of the
ancien régime, was also the least able to translate his political understanding
into specifically Christian language; he provided a political, but not a
religious substitute for Roman Catholicism.

Lamennais' withdrawal from Roman Catholicism into a religious position
not unlike that of David Strauss may have helped to stimulate the blanket
condemnation of Communism, Liberalism and Socialism which figured in
Pius IX's *Syllabus of Errors* (1864). The *Syllabus* made clear that traditional
Catholic ideas about the relation between the family and the state, and
between the state and the Church were not open to revision nor even,
essentially, to discussion. Pius IX refused to make any concessions to the
emerging secular and omnicompetent modern state which regarded the
Church as one more voluntary society to which it owed no other kind of
obligation than those which it recognized to all other voluntary societies.
This attitude did not die out in later nineteenth-century Catholicism; it
affected the way in which, in *Graves de Communi* (1901), Leo XIII distinguished between Social Democracy and Christian Democracy.

Social Democracy, he said, aimed at putting all government in the hands
of the people, reducing all ranks to the same level, abolishing all distinctions
of class, and introducing community of goods. The right of ownership was
to be abrogated, and whatever property a man possessed, or whatever
means of livelihood he had, was to be common to all. The acquirement and
enjoyment of corporal, external goods constituted the whole of man's
happiness. As against this, Christian Democracy, by the fact that it was
Christian, was necessarily built on the principles of the divine faith, and
provided for the betterment of the masses, with the ulterior object of
availing itself of the occasion to fashion their minds for things everlasting.
For Christian Democracy, justice was sacred; the right of acquiring and

possessing property could not be impugned; and the various distinctions and degrees which were indispensable to every well-ordered commonwealth must be safeguarded. Finally, Christian Democracy must try to preserve in every human society the form and character which God ceaselessly impressed upon it. Christian Democracy and Social Democracy had nothing in common. They differed as much as the sect of socialism differed from the profession of Christianity.

Christian Democracy, the encyclical continued, did not necessarily mean popular government, but simply a benevolent and Christian movement on behalf of the people. This statement has to be understood in the light of the earlier encyclical, *Rerum Novarum*, 'The condition of Labour' (1891). *Rerum Novarum*, still the foundation of modern Roman Catholic social theology, started from the assertion that 'some remedy must be found, and quickly found, for the misery and wretchedness which press so heavily on the large majority of the very poor'. The encyclical then dismissed the humanist remedy, socialism, as emphatically unjust, because socialist proposals would rob the lawful possessor, bring the state into a sphere which was not its own and cause complete confusion in the community.

In both papal pronouncements, property was seen as basic to the argument. *Rerum Novarum* said that when a man worked for money he did so in order to obtain property which he then wanted to keep in his private possession. Every man had by nature the right to property of his own: this was an appeal to natural law, which the socialists had no authority to disobey. The primary community in which this property-holding individual lived was the family, which was ideally and historically anterior to the state – a proposition which flatly contradicted the view of its own powers which the state had been developing steadily since the sixteenth century, and also ran counter to the Marxist thesis that neither family nor state had an extra-historical essence, but that both words could have very different meanings and mutual relations at different historical times. *Rerum Novarum* denounced the idea that class was naturally hostile to class; the contrary was the truth, for 'Capital cannot do without Labour, nor Labour without Capital', a statement that might have many different political meanings, and which could also be found in common use in various Protestant circles.

Rerum Novarum had no fresh insight into the causes of poverty. The encyclical relied on the view that the distribution of money depended upon the interplay of 'fortune' and 'misfortune'. That the poor might object to their poverty being interpreted as simply the result of uncontrollable chance did embarrass the authors, who said that as for those who did not possess the gifts of fortune, they were taught by the Church that in God's sight poverty was no disgrace and that there was nothing to be ashamed of in seeking one's bread by labour. There was also, however, a somewhat conflicting tendency to argue that infidelity and poverty were linked, for it was claimed that Christian morality, when it was adequately practised, conduced of itself to temporal prosperity, for it merited the blessing of God who was the source of all blessing. The Encyclical criticized those who wanted to replace charity with a system of state-organized relief: 'no human methods will ever supply the place of the devotion and self-sacrifice of Christian charity'.

The Encyclical concluded with practical proposals. Strikes, which were said to be normally harmful for all involved, were to be prevented as far as possible by removing the causes of conflict between employer and employee. Hours of labour should be regulated; children excluded from factories; women were not suited to certain trades, 'for a woman is by nature fitted for home-work'. Wages should be sufficient to support the wage-earner in reasonable and frugal comfort. If all this were done a new race of property-owning workers would arise, for if a workman's wages were sufficient to keep his family in reasonable comfort he would not find it hard, if he were a sensible man, to put by a little property. Such men had a natural right to form trade unions, and the state must protect natural rights. A Christian worker ought not to join a union run on principles incompatible with Christianity, and the Encyclical urged them to join the associations of Catholic employers and employees which it was one of Leo XIII's aims to promote.

It can be argued, and indeed in the long run it had to be argued, that *Rerum Novarum* was not meant to lay down rules from which a detailed Catholic policy could be worked out. Once again, as in the *Syllabus*, the Vatican was defining the relationship between the Church and the world. Capitalism was acceptable, as long as it conceded the workers' natural rights, which embraced a reasonable wage, good working conditions and unionization; socialism was not acceptable, if socialism meant the abolition of private property. Religion must take precedence over everything else as the only permanent foundation for a right relationship between capital and labour.

There was a wide gap between J. M. Ludlow's position, that the application of the Gospel to society required a new socio-economic structure, and the attempt of documents like *Rerum Novarum* to assimilate the modern industrial world and the mass urban society which it was producing to the hierarchical forms of organizations with which the churches had been familiar in the past. Many later nineteenth-century British and American Protestants, unwilling to ignore the poverty and misery of town life for the majority of people, nevertheless sided implicitly with the Encyclical in rejecting any demand for radical social change on theological grounds. Instead, they advocated the so-called Social Gospel: gambling, drinking and prostitution were denounced as the alleged causes of the troubles of the working-classes; enthusiastic, but not very successful, attempts were made to limit such behaviour. Protestant pietists seemed reluctant to look beyond symptoms and a moral judgement passed on individuals. They wanted the existing social order, but they wanted it administered in a tidier, more moralistic style. This was also the revivalist period *par excellence*, the age of Moody and Sankey, when many religious writers really thought that the working-man had only to will a change in his own behaviour, and largely ignored the extent to which individual conduct was enmeshed in an economic and social structure.

The social theology of two later nineteenth-century German writers,

Albrecht Ritschl (1822–89) and Wilhelm Herrmann (1846–1922) offered sophisticated examples of the negative way in which Protestant theology met the problems of a dynamic industrial society. For Ritschl, though he was a devoted admirer of Bismarck and the unified German Empire which he created, the state had no positive Christian function. The object of the state as such was order, the formation of an ethical community; this did not include the Christianization of the community, and one could not speak properly of either a Christian state, or of a Christian political party within a state. As the richest form of natural organization the state prepared men for the emergence of the Kingdom of God. This Kingdom, as Ritschl understood it, was a kind of international ethical-religious spiritual community which would express a world-wide consciousness of human solidarity. It was true that when this universal spiritual community had been established it would be clear that the theological understanding of history coincided with the history of European culture; non-European cultures had nothing to contribute beyond their capacity to enter into the western religious inheritance; but Ritschl was not aware of being a German nationalist, he regarded the idea of the Kingdom of God as the one safeguard against nationalism and other kinds of particularism. Perhaps his most striking statement of this idea was to be found in *Justification and Reconciliation*:

> Moral fellowship, viewed in these two characteristics of possessing the widest possible extension and being animated by the most comprehensive motive, can only be conceived as the Kingdom of God. This idea Christ expresses in such a way that He transcends the view of the national State, and takes up an attitude essentially opposed to it.[1]

Here was the basis of a radical Christian reply to the passionate nationalism of the nineteenth and twentieth centuries, but Ritschl was not as critical of Bismarckian Germany as his conception of the Kingdom of God might lead one to expect. Positively, he said that in post-1870 Germany Protestantism must transform the nation by forming a cultural community which would both strengthen the state and also lead onward to the Kingdom of God. At the same time, however, he attacked Social Democracy, Liberalism and Roman Catholic Ultramontanism (a comparison with the targets of the *Syllabus of Errors* is interesting) as destructive of the harmony of the new State. In 1887, not long before his death, he gave a famous public lecture in which he tried to show that these three groups did not oppose Bismarck as a matter of coincidence but were inspired by a common belief in natural law which they drew from medieval sources but which might also be traced back to pre-Christian times, a fact which Ritschl found especially damning. In effect, he made his own version of Protestant political conservatism the only possible Christian political stance, and showed little awareness of the importance of the 'social question' at all.

One reason why Ritschl related the modern state and the Kingdom of

[1] A. Ritschl, *Justification and Reconciliation*, ed. H. R. Mackintosh (New York, 1966), p. 252.

God so loosely together was that he combined a confidence in the divine
direction of human history with an optimistic faith in the possibilities of
nation-state behaviour – all this must somehow help to usher in the moral
integration of humanity in the Kingdom of God. As for the individual, he
said that 'moral action in our calling is the form in which our life-work as
a totality is produced as our contribution to the Kingdom of God'.[1] But he
had little to add to the eighteenth-century Lutheran downgrading of the
Reformation idea of vocation. 'A man's vocation', he said, 'as a citizen
denotes that particular department of work in human society in the
regular pursuit of which the individual realises at once his own self-end and
the ultimate end of society. Every civil vocation is an ethical vocation, and
not a means of egoism, in so far as it is pursued under the view that in
society as a whole and in the individual the moral law ought to be fulfilled,
and the highest conceivable goal for the race obtained. The varieties of
ethical vocation, according to their natural origin, divide themselves in
manifold fashion into vocations which have their origin in the family, those
which are concerned with the production, manipulation and distribution
of the means of the physical life, those connected with the state and with
religion, vocations in the sphere of science and art.'[2]

Ritschl's interpretation of vocation expressed only a vague sacralization
of the traditional order of things. It was all very well to make this the basis
of a moral integration of humanity into the divine kingdom, but men were
only likely to accept such a lofty spiritualization of human relationships if
they already accepted the social structure on which it rested, and in effect,
whether Ritschl recognized it or not, both the secular authority of the
European social order, which Marx had challenged, and its Christian status,
which writers like Ludlow had questioned, had declined in his lifetime.
For Ritschl himself, the decisive political events had been first, the failure
of the 1848 revolution in Prussia, after which he gave up his initial liberalism; and second, the triumph of Bismarck's drive to unite Germany
politically. He overvalued these events and the kind of unity which they
represented. As a result, he interpreted the evident alienation of the
German working-classes from the German Churches in the industrial
areas after 1850 as a breach of this new, and for him God-given, harmony.
His remedy was theological, not political, because as far as he could see
there was nothing political in the situation which he needed to repudiate.
What had alienated the working-class, he argued, was the Lutheran habit
of preaching about the consciousness of one's sinfulness to such a degree
that men felt that their work had no value in the eyes of God. Protestantism
must break out of this disastrous subjectivity, must accept and consecrate
the labours of mankind; if the Churches integrated the worker into their
own spiritual community he would soon find his place in the moralized
community of the state. In practice, however, it was the hard-working,
prosperous middle-class German Protestants who welcomed this change of
style and were pleased to see God's attention drawn to their contribution
to the new German Empire. Despite the potential critical power of his idea

[1] *ib.* p. 668.
[2] *ib.* p. 445.

of the Kingdom of God, then, Ritschl ended by asserting that the working-classes must adjust themselves spiritually as well as politically to the existing frame of society; he was as socially conservative as the popular apologists of the Social Gospel.

If Ritschl's theology expressed something of the widespread feeling in the western middle-classes that industrial expansion was not only good in itself but also a guarantee of the planet's future peace and prosperity, Wilhelm Herrmann, who had originally been a pupil of Ritschl's but in his later years broke with his master's ideas, gave expression to some of the doubts which were simultaneously arising in the same areas of society about what was happening. To some observers in the late nineteenth century it seemed not only that traditional values were being destroyed in the teeming cities of the west, where materialism apparently dominated, but also that the only effective new systems of value were those of socialism or marxism, which such observers identified with the denial of the existence of God, the abolition of private property and the rejection of the aesthetic standards of the past. In so far as he understood the situation in this way, Ritschl assumed that in a conflict between the spiritual and the material the spiritual would be bound to conquer, and he therefore opposed the view that Christianity necessarily implied or required any kind of withdrawal from the everyday, material world; the coming Kingdom of God would not turn out to be the justification of monasticism as the highest form of the Christian life.

In his later work, however, Herrmann stopped using the Kingdom of God as a theological category, and began to interpret the ethical commands of Christianity as world-renouncing. Herrmann attached great importance to ethical experience as such, because he regarded this as the ground on which modern religious belief could be rebuilt; he did not foresee, any more than similar liberal Protestant theologians like Tennant or Rashdall saw, that the authority of the so-called moral experience would soon be questioned as sharply as the authority of religious experience had been already. Herrmann, therefore, did not regard the 'social question' as important in itself – he was not a political theologian at all – but only as one more by-product of the inescapable inner struggle between the ethical-religious life of the individual man and the this-worldly demands of concrete living. The importance of Herrmann's position for social theology was that he changed what had come to be called *Kulturprotestantismus*, the Ritschlian desire to unite the spiritual and cultural, completely; his overriding interest in personal, and therefore individual, religious and moral experience destroyed the system as a theology of society at a time when some such social theology was, after all, desperately needed. Herrmann held that Christian ethics should be concerned with the inner spiritual growth of the individual, who should be led to see his primary ethical experience of life as an unsatisfactory conflict between world-renunciation and world-absorption, a conflict which could only be resolved beyond the sphere of the ethical in the sphere of the religious; the highest ethical achievement was open to man only as a divine gift. From this lofty height Herrmann explained the opposition of many Social Democrats to Christianity as the result of the personal life; the

proper business of the state was simply to protect and strengthen the
family, which formed the creative environment of both the ethical and
religious spheres.

Herrmann's view could be assessed in various ways. At one level he was
a religious existentialist who thought that men might best be persuaded to
return to religion if they first followed the path of ethical self-analysis to
what he took to be its inevitable end in shame and self-accusation. At the
level of social theology his attitude suggested that even at the beginning
of the twentieth century some Protestant theologians were still tempted to
think that the new industrial society offered no significantly altered situation for theology. An acute contemporary, Ernst Troeltsch (see p. 574), said
that Herrmann's theology still resembled much too closely the ethical
system of orthodox Lutheranism with its doctrine of the two realms and its
tendency to leave the responsibility for the context of human action to the
orders of creation. Herrmann's best-known book, *The Communion of the
Christian with God* (1886, 6th ed. 1908), was subtitled 'described on the
basis of Luther's statements', but he did not provide a satisfactory answer
to the question as to whether Luther's theology was relevant to the modern
world. This was not a question which came naturally to most Lutheran
theologians, but it came naturally enough to those who were not.

When one of the leaders of the next generation of German theologians,
Karl Barth, in *Protestant Theology in the Nineteenth Century* (1947), accused
Ritschl of subordinating the ideas of sin, justification, Christ and God to
the needs of man, so that for him Christianity seemed to exist simply in
order that the bourgeoisie should have the spiritual power and cultural
ease to enjoy the age of Bismarck with a good conscience, he was implying
that Ritschl was defending theologically the kind of Protestant self-
satisfaction which Kierkegaard had satirized in his *Attack on Christendom*
(1855). There was some truth in this, but Barth was not entirely fair to
either Ritschl or Herrmann, whom he regarded as typical figures of the
Liberal Protestantism which he himself was criticizing. For Ritschl
certainly distinguished between reconciliation as a religious activity fixed
in God, and ethical activity taking place in the sphere of personal relations;
he did not suppose that the busy middle-class was justified in God's sight
by its mere industriousness, or that the kingdom of God amounted to
nothing more than a perpetually expanding German Empire. And Herrmann, though more of a social individualist than Ritschl, and therefore
more justifiably criticized in this respect by Barth, drew back from any
identification of the purpose of man with the purpose of God, saying that
if men enjoyed the world they must do so as simultaneously standing apart
from it, having it as though they had it not. And in the 1920s Barth's own
political theology, with its strong impulse to leave the historical context to
the unchecked destructiveness of the political pseudo-creativity of man,
resembled that of Herrmann much more than he seems to have appreciated.

Nevertheless, the belief that modern western society rested on ideological
premises unacceptable to Christianity, and that there ought to be an alternative which was religiously preferable, grew steadily between the 1890s
and the end of the First World War, reaching its peak at the end of the

1920s. There were those in the English Anglo-Catholic tradition, for instance, who were so dismayed by the spectacle of mass industrialized society that they looked for a solution in a return to the past, to a medieval Christian model of society, an approach which had little positive result because it was so divorced from reality. A. J. Penty, for example, in an essay called 'The Obstacle of Industrialism', anticipated a time when once again agriculture and craftsmanship (in a very limited sense) would be exalted as the foundation of national prosperity, and when a Just and Fixed Price would be maintained by a system of Guilds covering the country (*The Return of Christendom*, by a Group of Churchmen, 1922).

Others, like the American Baptist, Walter Rauschenbusch (1861–1918), whose work was another comment on the popular but muddled belief that the weakness of Liberal Protestantism lay in its excessive individualism, sought to develop the Ritschlian system from its original form. One of the key chapters of Rauschenbusch's best-known book, *Christianity and the Social Crisis* (1907), was headed 'The Social Aims of Jesus', and concluded:

> Jesus has been called the first socialist. He was more; he was the first real man, the inaugurator of a new humanity. But as such he bore within him the germs of a new social and political order ... Theologians have felt no hesitation in founding a system of speculative thought on the teachings of Jesus, and yet Jesus was never an inhabitant of the realm of speculative thought. He has been made the founder and organiser of a great ecclesiastical machine, which derives authority for its offices and institutions from him, and yet 'hardly any problem of exegesis is more difficult than to discover in the gospels an administrative or organizing or ecclesiastical Christ'. There is at least as much justification in invoking his name today as the champion of a great movement for a more righteous social life. He was neither a theologian, nor an ecclesiastic, nor a socialist. But if we were forced to classify him either with the great theologians ... or with the mighty popes and princes of the Church ... or with the men who are giving their heart and life to the propaganda of a new social system – where should we place him?[1]

Rauschenbusch's emphasis fell on the need to abolish the competitive and individualistic socio-economic order. Primitive society, he said, was 'communistic'. So were the most valuable institutions in the modern world, the family, school and Church. Even the state was essentially 'communistic', and was now becoming more so. Rauschenbusch insisted that Christianity had more in common with cooperative systems than with competitive disunity; it ought to help society to evolve from the existing phase of economic individualism to a higher kind of community. And since idealists alone were unable to change the world, Christianity should ally itself with the working-classes; once they controlled the means of production, industry could be reorganized on the basis of cooperation; this was the first vital step to the Christianization of the social order.

There was, of course, no serious question of the early twentieth-century

[1] See *The Social Gospel in America*, ed. R. T. Handy (1966).

American Churches supporting the under-organized American proletariat
in a campaign to storm the heights of American capitalism. Teetotalism
was closer to the Protestant heart, and the women's suffrage movement
benefited from the belief that women, if given the vote, would use it against
the liquor interest. Yet Rauschenbusch put his finger on the problem which
was to dominate political theology for the next seventy years. Should
organized Christianity simply be content to try to moralize the economic
status quo; should it work for a radical reform of society in the not so
distant future; or, going beyond Rauschenbusch's immediate horizon,
should it support potentially violent revolutionary groups which were
committed to seizing power? Behind this lay another, older distinction
between those theologians who interpreted history pessimistically, believing
that human society would steadily deteriorate until the abrupt return of
Christ brought secular history to an end; and those who believed that both
Church and Society would steadily grow better and better until an age of
perfect peace and prosperity painlessly ushered in the Second Coming.
With the aid of the historical-critical method Rauschenbusch unhesitatingly
recruited Jesus for the second point of view.

> Jesus, like all the prophets and like all his spiritually minded country-
> men, lived in the hope of a great transformation of the national, social
> and religious life about him. He shared the substance of that hope with
> his people, but by his profounder insight and his loftier faith he elevated
> and transformed the common hope. He rejected all violent means and
> thereby transferred the inevitable conflict from the field of battle to
> the antagonism of mind against mind . . . He postponed the divine
> catastrophe of judgement to the dim distance and put the emphasis
> on the growth of the new life that was now going on . . . The tone of
> sadness in his later ministry was not due simply to the approach of his
> own death but to the consciousness that his purpose for his nation had
> failed . . . He began then to draw his disciples more closely about him
> and to create the nucleus of a new nation within the old . . . He also
> rose then to the conviction that he would return and accomplish in the
> future what he had hoped to accomplish in this earthly life.[1]

This Jesus was saddened by events, rejected by the society to which he
came, yet still determined to create a new life for mankind – the catastrophe
of judgement was postponed into the distant future. This picture reflected
Rauschenbusch's own situation. He had published a programme called
'Practical Socialism' in 1901, precisely on the ground that the revolution
for which the doctrinaire socialists were waiting would take a long time to
come, and that it was immoral to put off reform in the present for the sake
of changes which might or might not happen in the future. He suggested,
among other schemes, the municipalization of electricity, gas and water;
the extension of local education; library and museum services; and an
inheritance tax. This might have been regarded as 'Fabianism' in the
England of the same period, and one should distinguish between 'social
gospel' as the name for a kind of moral crusade about behaviour (drinking,

[1] W. Rauschenbusch, *Christianity and the Social Crisis* (1907), pp. 65–6.

gambling, etc.), and 'social gospel' as the name for programmes which were more concerned with altering the social environment and less with personal behaviour.[1]

In Germany, events moved faster than in America, as was to be expected in a country where even before 1914 the Social Democratic Party had become a powerful organ of opposition to the Prussian idea of a united Germany. Harnack attached importance to the problem of what was to be done to re-integrate the social-democratic world into the general community and in this he was more realistic than Herrmann; the move away from the more moralistic version of the Social Gospel (which had its German equivalent, the 'evangelisch-sozial') came at the opening of the twentieth century. The first new leader was C. F. Blumhardt (1842–1919), who in late middle-age emerged as the centre of what was called a movement of 'Religious Socialism'. He was the mildest of the group; he used biblical language to paint a picture of God coming near to the poor and wretched in the Kingdom; he taught that Jesus had planted a seed in the human race which had grown among the Jews and atheists as well as among the Christians; the socialist utopia was therefore itself an offshoot of the Kingdom of God. Blumhardt sat as a social-democratic member of the Württemberg Diet from 1900 to 1906, whereas the British Free Church ministers who sat in Parliament in the Edwardian period did so as members of the Liberal Party. Even before the outbreak of war in 1914 the Religious Socialists were moving on to more dramatic statement, however; one of Blumhardt's associates, the Swiss theologian, Hermann Kütter, said in 1912, that the Social Democrats were revolutionary because God was revolutionary; they were men of revolution because God was the great revolutionary; the Religious Socialists must advance with them because so must the Kingdom of God.

Fundamental to Religious Socialism was the idea which Paul Tillich developed after 1918, that the Christian faith was a response to the Christ-event which, once freed from the narrowing effects of confessionalism which helped to bind men to their own social and economic self-interest, required and also made possible a comprehensive understanding of the will of God for society. This meant that the traditional opposition between the Church and the world was replaced by the idea of confrontation between God and his whole creation, the Church being regarded in its institutional form as one of the varieties of human rebellion against God. This was originally a point of agreement between Tillich and Karl Barth, who began his career close to the Religious Socialists, and with a similar impulse to criticise the visible Church. The political controversy about the proper economic form of society had added detail and sophistication to the traditional attack on the Church for becoming too involved in 'the world', a tradition which reached Barth, for example, through Kierkegaard.

Barth, however, refused to support the Christian Labour movement which the Religious Socialists wanted to start among the proletariat; he said

---

[1] See P. d'A. Jones, *The Christian Socialist Revival 1877–1914* (Princeton, 1968), for an account of how the later Christian Socialists failed, by and large, to set out a distinctively *christian* socialism.

that his earlier attacks on the Church had been 'churchly', not 'anti-church', that they had been made from a stance consciously *inside* the Church and with no intention of seeking to supersede what existed. Barth was perhaps less moved by the political upheavals which followed the German loss of the war in 1918 than was Tillich. For Tillich the post-war years in Germany seemed to present a chance to realize the evangelical principle in the specific social-democratic case now that the whole nation had fallen into what he interpreted as a revolutionary situation. Theologians have tended to agree with Barth in dismissing Tillich and the Religious Socialists as misguided, and certainly theologians cannot hope to manipulate the Church into doing politically what the majority of its members do not actually want to do. Nevertheless, the historical conclusion of the 1920s was the victory of Adolf Hitler, and this suggests that Tillich's campaign to persuade the German Churches to accept a socialist Weimar – which many German Catholics and Protestants were loath to do, whether for religious, nationalist, or anti-marxist reasons – was politically justifiable. The survival of Weimar was hardly the worst that could have happened. Barth, despite his theoretical approval of the Social Democratic Party, an approval which he maintained after 1933 on the ground that the Party stood for the working-class and for the German anti-militarist tradition, took little or no part in Social Democratic affairs during the Weimar Republic's short lease of Germany. On the other hand, when Tillich said in 1919 that the Religious Socialists stood on the ground of the Socialist Revolution, as distinct from the 'evangelisch-sozial' position, he was bound to antagonize many in the German Churches.

It is enlightening to look at the different approaches of Ludlow, Kütter, Tillich, and the later Czech Protestant leader, Josef Hromadka (1889–1969), to the problem of a Christian politics. What affected Ludlow most deeply, for example, was not the sufferings of the working-classes but the way in which a section of the commercial classes bought cheap, sold dear and claimed that wages ought to be settled in the same non-moral atmosphere: he lived at a time when social reformers still hoped to modify the attitudes of the possessing groups, and before pseudo-Darwinian images of 'struggle' and 'survival' had increased the total effect of Malthus on the early Victorian imagination. Kütter, when he published *Sie Müssen* in 1904, no longer believed that it was possible to educate the forces which he collectively labelled 'Mammon'; he felt that the oppressive behaviour of capitalist society justified revolution to the extent that Christians could not oppose it in the name of order or decency or the will of God; he wrote as though revolution was historically inevitable, as though the proletariat would certainly be victorious, and as though what mattered therefore was the attitude which the Churches adopted to the new order which was coming. God was on the side of the revolution, because this revolution would be for the sake of His people, the poor and the helpless. Going much further than either Ludlow or his successors in England, Kütter said: 'The class war exists. It was there from the first moment that the oppressed lay at the foot of the oppressor' (*Sie Müssen*, p. 111). Mammon was to blame for the class struggle; strikes were justifiable because the employing class made concessions only under duress. The whole argument is interesting, because it was to recur, *mutatis mutandis*, after the Second World War with relation to the Third World, and especially to South America, where minority Catholic theologians defended Christian involvement in a struggle for economic, social and cultural liberation in very similar terms. (See G. Gutiérrez, *A Theology of Liberation* (1973); H. Assmann, *Practical Theology of Liberation* (1973); and J. M. Bonino, *Revolutionary Theology Comes of Age* (1975).) Throughout the twentieth century, in fact, the problem of the Christian attitude to violence as a political method was never far from the mind of the sophisticated theologian.

For all his fire, however, Kütter in 1904 did not really expect that revolution would happen soon. In 1919, on the other hand, Tillich believed for a moment that revolution had taken place. He therefore repeated Kütter's argument that the Churches should side with the revolution, but the slow collapse of Weimar, like the weakness of the far from revolutionary British socialist governments in 1923 and 1929, showed that the Russian Revolution had not after all heralded the total disintegration of western capitalism. And as the Nazi movement tightened its hold on Germany the Christian groups were forced into so negative a position that Dietrich Bonhoeffer seriously considered the place of the assassination of Hitler in a Christian programme.

For Hromadka the historical circumstances were different again. Tillich had soon to face the fact that the Germany of the 1920s was not going to become a socialist state. Hromadka, however, quickly realized that the Communist takeover in Czechoslovakia in 1948 would last his lifetime, which it did. By the end of the 1950s, he said, the structure of the socialist state had been consolidated; not even those most opposed to socialism still believed that it would be possible, by force or by secret infiltration, to liquidate the new political order. But for that very reason Czech Protestants faced a complex question of what to do in order that the individual might become a convinced and responsible partner in the building of the new society, and so that he might bring to it everything from the Protestant past and from that of the rest of the world which had helped to raise the level and dignity of human life. There must therefore be a Christian-Marxist dialogue which would cover not only questions of philosophical theology, but also the Marxist and Christian attitudes to the deep social divisions of human society. The class struggle, Hromadka said, was not just a slogan, but pointed to the gap between riches and poverty, whether in individuals or nations.[1] There were signs of such a dialogue beginning in France in the 1960s, between writers as distinguished as the Roman Catholic theologian, Karl Rahner, and Roger Garaudy, at one time a prominent member of the French Communist Party, but who was expelled in 1970.[2] In his *Theological Investigations* (volume XII, 1974) Karl Rahner insisted that political theology was still in its infancy, that the task of criticizing society which belonged to the official Church had still not achieved any theological definition. There was no absolute political

[1] J. L. Hromadka, *Thoughts of a Czech Pastor* (1970), p. 90.
[2] See R. Garaudy, *The Turning-Point of Socialism* (1969) and *The Whole Truth* (1971).

theology. A social encyclical like *Mater et Magistra* (1961) was not doctrine or binding prescription, but something that was recommended to the historically created freedom of man. He accepted much of the criticism of the visible Church. Where the Church was not directly threatened by the institutions of the society and the state, he said, and where the leaders of Christian thought did not feel themselves directly injured by institutionalized injustice, the task of the Church as a social critic was largely neglected. The case of South America was not far from Rahner's mind, and he recalled that Pius XI, in *Firmissiman Constantiam* (1937) had said that when a social order threatened the ultimate basis of human living and rights, revolutionary force might not only be permitted but even prescribed to Christians. Rahner said that *Spes et Gaudium*, a social document from the second Vatican Council, accepted that there might be complete political disagreement between groups of conscientious Christians, and implied that although in such situations individual groups could not claim the authority of the official Church, they could appeal to the authority of the Gospel.[1] There was no question here of a reconciliation of the Catholic and Marxist understandings of Man and God; Rahner was suggesting, however, that in the political area at least (and this included issues like education policy and toleration) the claims of revelation could be defended and discussed without the intransigeance of the *Syllabus of Errors*: doctrinal and political pluralism were not impossible from his point of view. For Rahner the Church was one social group within a pluralistic society; even natural law did not yield absolutely unreserved and concrete imperatives such as would deprive man and society of the power to commit themselves to historical decisions, in other words, to change things. The recognition that cultures have histories has profoundly affected Catholic social theology, so that the rôle assigned to property in *Rerum Novarum*, for example, might now be thought of as a historical case, rather than necessarily as a normative proposition.[2]

As for Britain, the Christian Socialist tradition did not collapse overnight after the First World War. It was still possible in 1923 for an official Anglican committee on 'Christianity and Industrial Problems', for example, to report that the fundamental evil of modern industrialism was that it encouraged competition for private gain instead of co-operation for public service. This perversion of motive, the Report said, fostered an organization of industry which treated the workers as hands rather than persons. This encouraged conditions of poverty which did not arise from the personal defects of individuals or from natural scarcity, but which existed side by side with excessive riches. There was an attitude of mutual antagonism and suspicion between the different parties engaged in industry. And it stated categorically that the concept of industry as a selfish competitive struggle was unchristian. Industry ought to be regarded primarily as a social service, based on the effort of every individual to discharge his duty to his neighbour and the community.[3] The Committee recommended the

---

[1] K. Rahner, *Theological Investigations*, vol. 12 (1974), p. 246.
[2] K. Rahner, *Theological Investigations*, vol. 14 (1976), 'The Unreadiness of the Church's members to Accept Poverty', pp. 270–79, is a good example.
[3] E. Talbot, ed., *Christianity and Industrial Problems* (1918), pp. 50–74.

principle of a living wage, unemployment insurance, and the setting up of an industrial parliament to represent the statesmanship of all parties in industry, an idea which recurred steadily down to 1939, especially in circles influenced by corporatist theories.

This condemnation of the spirit of capitalism was reminiscent of Maurice's denunciation of the assertion that competition was a law of the universe, but the Report said little about the structure of industry. This was because the Committee was chiefly moved (as the Christian Socialists had been in 1848) by a sense of the alienation of the working-classes from organized religion. The 1916 Report on *Church and State* had said that the hostility of the working-class originated partly in the belief that the Church was the moral policeman that the propertied classes used to protect their own interests, and partly in the belief that the moral teaching of the Church was against progress, and social change.[1] Apart from asking for more working-class priests (but not suggesting how they could be found if the case was as stated) the later *Report* advocated improved education, including a *compulsory* scheme for half-time school attendance by factory-workers between the age when full-time schooling stopped and that of eighteen; it was high-handed as well as high-minded.[2]

Between 1918 and 1939 the Anglican and Roman Churches in Britain suffered from a conflict between the recognition that organized Christianity had really very little influence on what happened in industry (as was clear in the General Strike of 1926), and a conviction that they ought as Churches to play a reconciling rôle in society. This was the social theology of the majority of the clergy (not social radicalism), who always thought of themselves as exercising a ministry of reconciliation in a static but disharmonious world. They could not believe that the real world of the inter-war years was in flux, and that the majority of the laity thought that the official Churches should not play an independent political rôle on the basis of an allegedly Christian programme.

William Temple (1881–1944), who was Archbishop of Canterbury for the last two years of his life, was therefore perhaps unduly optimistic when, between 1941 and 1944 he tried to form what he called 'a body of influence guided by Christian principles' to plead in the post-war period for aims such as proper housing and adequate nutritional standards for the whole nation. Temple believed that the Church had the right to lay down the principles which should govern the ordering of human society, because the Church possessed a divine revelation which illuminated every phase of human conduct. It was the ease with which such generalizations could be translated into 'principles' which was growing old-fashioned, and the post-war period in fact offered evidence for the mutability of 'Christian principles' when, in 1958, for example, the Lambeth Conference finally abandoned the position that artificial contraception could be permitted only in cases of exceptional social or medical need; instead, a case was now made for 'positive parenthood', which meant the 'planned family'. It was even

[1] *Report of the Archbishops' Committee on Church and State* (1916), p. 253.
[2] See E. R. Norman, *Church and Society in England 1770–1970* (1976), for a discussion of the influence of class-background on Anglican social thinking.

stated in 'The Family in Contemporary Society' that 'those who carelessly
and improvidently bring children into the world trusting in an unknown
future or a generous society to care for them, need to make a vigorous
examination of their lack of concern for their children and for the society
of which they are a part'.[1] Although the Lambeth Committee produced an
exposition of *Genesis* which justified the change of view, this was a kind of
ingenuity which only underlined the historically relative nature of the shift
in policy. And this throws light on the demand for 'theologians of revolution': it is the post-revolutionary period which matters most, and at that
point the dogmatist, whether religious or secular, has become obsolete.[2]

In general, then, the second half of the twentieth century has not seen
the formulation of an agreed social theology. This is hardly surprising when
one remembers that industrial societies have themselves been sharply
divided by rival theories of the ideal state. Theologians who believe that
Christian institutions should seek to foster social reconciliation in terms of
the existing system instead of supporting social conflict in terms of some
possible future system naturally do not want to choose between (for
example) capitalism and socialism, and their position relates easily to those
passages in the New Testament which reflect the early Christian acceptance
of the hierarchical society of the Roman Empire in which the new religious
movement came to life. The christians of the first five centuries did not
consciously set out to turn the Mediterranean world upside down in a socio-
political sense. They inhabited a culture in which critical groups often
contracted out; fourth and fifth century monks and hermits, for example,
expressed by withdrawal a widespread intellectual distaste for what they
regarded as a decadent urban way of life. In the twentieth century the loss
of social power by religious institutions, their inability to prevent, for
instance, secular legal systems from developing an attitude to marriage
which ignores ecclesiastical tradition, has increased the attractiveness of
this kind of theology, which should not be confused with the kind of
political conservatism which uses classical Christian pessimism about human
nature as a justification for the rejection of socialism. Opposition to political
activity may spring (as it did in Karl Barth's case in the 1920s) from a
profound insight into the possible rôle of the Christian community as the
symbol of the coming Kingdom of God; Christians, Barth thought, should
not commit themselves either to the political left or the political right, as
though one or other of these secular political attitudes embodied the divine
society in its programme. God worked out his purposes through his own
people, whose loyalty to him must transcend other loyalties of whatever
kind.

Barth's point of view must be distinguished not only from the neo-
Hegelian long-haul optimism of the older versions of the 'social gospel', as
well as from the more desperate social eschatology of the 'revolutionary'
Christians of the 1970s, but also from the so-called 'Christian realism' of the
American theologian, Reinhold Niebuhr (1892–1971), who rejected the

[1] The Lambeth Conference, 1958, Report 5, 'The Family in Contemporary Society',
Part 2, p. 146.
[2] See Hugo Assmann, *Practical Theology of Liberation* (1975), pp. 143–44.

political idealism of Rauschenbusch and his successors, which seemed to him only political innocence, not least in the context of totalitarianism. It might even be said of Niebuhr that his latent criterion of Christian political thinking was its degree of political success; it was certainly part of his criticism of the Christian social radicals that they often seemed to make almost a cult of political failure. His social theology was contained in *Moral Man and Immoral Society* (1932), *An Interpretation of Christian Ethics* (1935) and *Christian Realism and Political Problems* (1954). Niebuhr combined a sense of sin which tempted him to political cynicism, and therefore to an overeasy acceptance of power politics and concepts like the Cold War, with a religious perfectionism which prompted a desire for social change and led him to reintroduce those ideas of moral and social 'progress' against which he had reacted in his earlier books. Niebuhr was able to see through the naiveté of much of the idealistic ecclesiastical political talk and action which abounded in the 1930s; but his cult of 'realism' did not prove as reliable a guide after 1950, when the United States was drifting towards total engagement in Vietnam as well as into urban and racial chaos. Both Barth and Niebuhr approached politics from the orthodox side of the nineteenth-century theological tradition; both saw the danger of assuming that speculations about the continuity and coherence of history – whether idealist or materialist – formed part of the Christian understanding of man and his existence; both were well aware of the temptation, institutional as well as individual, to read politics into religion and come to absolute conclusions. Both, however, accepted the view that major theologians must make political pronouncements. Perhaps neither fully appreciated the position which Rahner was to hold in the 1960s, that even the deepest theological insight would not yield absolute political imperatives such as would deprive men and society of the power to commit themselves to decisions in history: politics was not a simple material to be moulded with a few unchanging principles.

Nevertheless, theologians of society had certainly not retreated to the static theology of the *ancien régime*. Positions had in fact been modified in the second half of the twentieth century. Social change was still theologically accepted; what had slackened was belief in the immediate future. The revolutionary myth, secular as well as theological, had lost some of its potency for the first time since 1789. Theologians tended to invoke the eschatological language and imagery of the Bible, the promise of a final divine intervention, in order to assert that at least the conclusion of history would make moral and religious sense. Many western marxist intellectuals were just as unhappy about the present age, seeming to have lost faith in the revolutionary potential of the working-classes. Secular society itself had lost some of its enchantment, and although monasticism had collapsed as a serious alternative way of life, it seemed as though a new theology of withdrawal was in the air, a spiritual withdrawal of consent from the contemporary organization of man. Such views neither repeated nor endorsed any previous theology, and lacked authoritative formulation; but the tide of secularization, which had run so strongly throughout the period which has been discussed here, seemed checked or turned. It is true that there was still disagreement in the 1970s as to whether the Christian Churches either could or should support violent or non-violent political action against the existing regimes in parts of the world like South Africa or South America; but this was only a symptom of a more subtle theological disengagement from some of the assumptions which had come to dominate modern industrial, urban, nationalist and aggressive society.

V

THE TWENTIETH CENTURY

Granted that at the beginning of the twentieth century traditional doctrines seemed more than usually in question, there were still those theologians who were prepared to defend the orthodox position. In England, for instance, Darwell Stone (1859–1941) advanced an unmodified High Anglican theology in his *Outlines of Christian Dogma* (1900); while P. T. Forsyth (1848–1921) made a brave reaffirmation of the Reformed position in such books as *The Person and Place of Jesus Christ* (1909), though his *The Christian Ethic of War* (1916), a passionate attack on conscientious objection as the evil fruit of a generation of theological liberalism, showed that traditionalism was just as subject to the pressures of circumstances as liberalism was said to have been.

If such writers were not very influential, one reason was that the problems which theologians were being called upon to solve were changing. Late nineteenth-century Protestant theological systems still centred on the individual. One can illustrate this in the case of popular religion, where the American Ira D. Sankey's once famous *Sacred Songs and Solos* (1873 onwards) exploited for revivalism such themes as the anxious, loving father who waited patiently for the return of his repentant 'wandering boy', whom he would then forgive and restore to all the joys of 'home'; and in the case of more formal theology, in the example of Ritschl, for whom the individual's moral experience formed the core of the anti-ontological theology which, as Paul Tillich said, provided a theological foundation for the growth of the strong, active, morally disciplined bourgeois individual of the period.[1] Both attitudes implied a definite relaxation of the intensity with which Soeren Kierkegaard had passionately restated Christianity in terms of an individual who alone could achieve the impossibly absolute relation to the Absolute. In *The Social Teaching of the Christian Churches* (1912, E.T. 1931), Ernst Troeltsch described Christian history largely as a permanent tension between 'the idealistic anarchy and love-communism, which with radical indifference or antipathy toward the other orders of the world embodies the love-idea in small circles', and a socially conservative tradition which preferred some kind of adaptation to the existing social order;[2] but he went on to argue that in the twentieth century both the world-accommodating Church and the world-denying Sect had become intolerable to the educated mind, for whom the religious institution remained possible only in the form

[1] P. Tillich, *Perspectives on Protestant Theology* (1967), pp. 215–19.
[2] E. Troeltsch, *Social Teaching of the Christian Churches* (1931), p. 75.

of the liberal protestant voluntary association.[1] Nietzsche's piercing cry
that God was dead made no impact on the theologians who replied to him:
J. N. Figgis (1866–1919), for example, in *The Will to Freedom* (1917).
Kierkegaard might have understood Nietzsche, but his influence was still
to come.

The First World War made a tremendous impact on a generation which
had inherited a theology of evil, guilt, repentance and forgiveness conceived
on a domestic scale for individual people. The war in France sickened aud
exhausted men beyond what they could either endure or interpret through
their traditional Roman Catholic or Protestant world-views. It was the
experience of many men that the normal springs of religious confidence,
religious belief and religious feeling perished under such violent pressure.
The question of God's existence, of the possibility and credibility of religious experience, seemed much more important than questions of personal
guilt, repentance and divine forgiveness. The Stalinist terror, the Nazi
persecution of the Jews, the dropping of atomic bombs on Japan, the bitter
conflicts in Algeria and the destruction in Vietnam after 1945, all prolonged
the reaction, and seemed to exceed the human capacity to find face-saving
explanations for God's apparent tolerance of evil. The old theological appeal
to human free will as a moral explanation of such events had worn thin
after 1914, when a British officer could write, after the Somme battle, which
was the real turning-point of feeling in that war:

> It did not seem possible that a gentleman could abandon, so fully as
> Providence appeared to have done, his servants to the cruelties of the
> world, on the specious ground that human agency must have a free
> hand. Except ye believe (not serve) Me, ye shall in no wise enter my
> Kingdom – a harsh threat, I thought, that no gentleman would utter
> to any servitor who, not in this world of his own accord, nevertheless
> carried out his duties to the best of his ability, maybe giving his life
> for them.[2]

In its fascist and marxist forms, totalitarianism also helped to make men
feel that what was happening showed that the universe had no sort of
underlying purposive structure: existence had no meaning beyond what
men arbitrarily imposed themselves.[3] In an essay, 'Can a truly contemporary person not be an atheist?', Dr. J. A. T. Robinson included, as part
of a threefold argument, the assertion that God was morally intolerable. He
linked together writers like Feuerbach, Proudhon, Nietzsche, Dostoievsky,
Camus and Sartre and said that this variety of atheism drew its strength
from the seriousness with which it took the problem of evil: Camus' novel,
The Plague (1947), a study of innocent suffering, spoke for a whole
generation.[4]

If the theologians failed to cope with the task of explaining the ways of
God to man, part of the trouble lay in their inability to absorb the scientific

[1] *ib.* p. 381.
[2] J. Terraine, ed., *General Jack's Diary 1914–18* (1964), p. 158.
[3] See the writings of Hannah Arendt, especially *Between Past and Future* (1961).
[4] J. A. T. Robinson, *The New Reformation?* (1965), p. 112.

understanding of biological evolution into the pattern of classical Christian orthodoxy. In a popular account of nineteenth-century church history, for example, A. R. Vidler said that by about 1890 'theologians, at least in the universities, were no longer making reluctant concessions to advances in the natural sciences but were claiming them almost as a godsend', and he quoted the totally undarwinian view of Aubrey Moore (1849–90), a theologian in the anglo-catholic tradition, that 'apart from the scientific evidence in favour of evolution, as a theory it is infinitely more Christian than the theory of special creation'.[1] This apparent acceptance of evolutionary theory often amounted to no more than the adoption of a pre-Darwinian, Enlightenment belief that history, now defined so as to include the biological pre-history of man and the other forms of life, revealed a process of development in which Spirit progressively dominated matter, and it was precisely this easy commerce with teleology which crumpled in the twentieth century. An Anglican anthropologist of the Edwardian period, W. H. L. Duckworth, for instance, said that 'the past history of man fails to reveal to scientists the evidence of a sudden degradation like that implied in the expression "fall". On the contrary, the general tendency has been upwards, though the path has been by no means straight, deviations have been numerous and mistakes frequent.'[2] Here at least the optimism was qualified, but the Scottish theologian, Henry Drummond (1851–97), imagined that in the evolutionary process the altruistic struggle for the life of others (as he called it) emerged from the primitive struggle for existence and became the over-rising impulse:

> In that new social order which the gathering might of the altruistic spirit is creating now around us, in that reign of love which must one day, if the course of evolution hold on its way, be realised, the baser elements will find that solvent prepared for them from the beginning in anticipation of a higher rule on earth . . . Evolution is nothing but the Involution of Love, the revelation of Infinite Spirit, the Eternal Life returning to itself.[3]

Drummond's rhetoric has become unreadable with time, but it is interesting to compare his optimism with a much later discussion of the doctrine of the fall of man:

> Now it is in this sense that man is fallen. Man has innate a genius (they call it the image of God), a genius for absolute generosity which is the essence of goodness. But as yet man cannot fully actualise this genius. He cannot give himself as he knows he has it in himself to give himself. *This is not his fault.* He was born that way. But, none the less, it makes him fall short of his full stature. He is fallen from what in God's Providence he one day will be.[4]

Here 'providence' is the dominating Spirit, man the malleable creature. Drummond's real heir, however, was Teilhard de Chardin (1881–1955) the

[1] A. R. Vidler, *The Church in an Age of Revolution* (1961), p. 121.
[2] H. B. Swete, ed., *Cambridge Theological Essays* (1905), p. 173.
[3] H. Drummond, *The Ascent of Man* (1894), pp. 45–6.
[4] H. A. Williams, *The True Wilderness* (1965).

Jesuit priest and scientist, who injected a similarly optimistic note into his highly speculative application of the idea of a evolutionary process to the universe as a whole. Teilhard, however, was not representative of the Roman Catholic position: until the first decade of the twentieth century the theory of evolution was almost unanimously rejected by theologians: a decree of the Biblical Commission of 1909 still said that a special creation of the first man was to be held as the literal historical sense of the second chapter of the book of Genesis.[1]

The most positive attempt made in the early twentieth century to combine biology and the Christian tradition was contained in *The Origin and Propagation of Sin* by F. R. Tennant (1866–1957). Tennant rejected the traditional Christian pessimism about man, as it had been developed from the Bible, especially from the combination of Genesis with the Pauline epistles. He assumed that the story about Adam and Eve and the serpent was a theologically irrelevant fragment of folklore, the exact intention of which it was impossible to decide. Instead, he appealed from the Scriptures understood in the light of tradition to the evidence of the evolutionary process as he was aware of it. This process seemed to him to have produced man as originally an impulse-governed, lawless organism, fulfilling the nature necessarily his and therefore the life which God willed for him, a man who could not therefore accurately be called 'rebellious'. (The idea of man as 'rebellious' was to be strongly revived in the 1920s by Karl Barth and Emil Brunner: later still, Barth was to call Adam 'the man who sinned at once', who was no sooner man at all than he was also proud man, in rebellion against God.)[2]

In this original man the moral consciousness awakened only slowly – there was no question of some catastrophic change for the worse in his relationship with God, nor was there, at a later stage in man's development, a 'radical bias towards evil' because of the Fall. Tennant was not unreasonably irritated when critics accused him of explaining sin and its sinfulness away, when in fact he made the process of moral growth, which in itself inevitably involved a constantly more acute sense of the nature of evil, the fundamental theme in the story of humanity. 'The sinfulness of sin', he wrote, 'is really more stoutly maintained by a theory which makes all sin actual and a matter of personal accountability, however less guilty its earlier stages may be than its later, than by a theory which finds the source of sinfulness in a supposed hereditary state for which no person is accountable'.[3]

Tennant absolutized the moral sense (in the Victorian fashion) by attributing its awakening directly to God. The Infinite was immanent in each human being and the phenomena of man's sensitive life were due to his agency. Tennant, however, stopped short of the panentheism which the idea of evolution in its broadest sense had made popular on the Continent; instead, he asserted the reality of man's finite freedom. In his *Philosophical Theology* he defended an ethical theism 'which takes the realisation of

[1] See K. Rahner, *Hominisation* (1965), p. 29.
[2] K. Barth, *Church Dogmatics*, vol. 4, *The Doctrine of Reconciliation*, Part 1, pp. 358–514.
[3] F. R. Tennant, *The Origin and Propagation of Sin* (2 ed. 1908), Preface, p. xx.

personality and moral values to be the raison d'être of the world',[1] and this ethical theism was also the basic presupposition of his Christian theology. God revealed the ideal, prepared the heart, supplied the inspiration, but the activity which in human response warred against 'the flesh' – by which Tennant understood the natural and essential, and in themselves not immoral, instincts and impulses of man's animal ancestors – was man's own. Certainly, man was divided, his animal basis conflicting with his acquired human conscience, but the traditional theological question as to how such discord could arise in human life when everything pointed to its proper condition as one of unity and harmony rested (in Tennant's view) on an incorrect presupposition, on the preconception that man had been created at a single stroke both intelligent and elementarily moral, without the background of any prior development. Tennant was quite ready to tolerate the picture of man which he believed followed from the data supplied by modern western science: he regarded 'human nature' as a variable, flowing quality, indefinable in any classical, once-for-all sense. It was as true to say that God was still making man as to say that God had made him, and the origin and meaning of sin had similarly to be sought in the process of becoming.

Nor did Tennant accept the theory which was expressed in several contemporary reviews of *The Origin and Propagation of Sin*, that the 'myth' of the creation of man in the book of Genesis still contained the material for a proper doctrine of human nature. What, Tennant asked very reasonably, was the test of the validity of a doctrine derived from it? Was it the alleged divine inspiration of the story? There would seem to be no other possible guarantee that the narrative of the 'Fall' supplied what might be called a set of theological facts. But, Tennant objected, 'we must define inspiration in this connexion in the light of an inquiry into whether that which the narrative asserts is positive fact, rather than assume its assertions to be true because they occur in the pages of a book which we regard as inspired'.[2] He also rejected the attempt made by such writers as Aubrey Moore to salvage the prestige of Genesis by arguing that the evidence of history showed that one was bound to assume a permanent bias toward evil in human nature. In the preface to the 1908 edition he wrote:

I am aware that because, from the first dawning of his knowledge of what he ought to do, every human being has failed always to avoid doing what he has known he ought not to do, some philosophers as well as theologians have attributed a 'bias' to the human will, or spoken of 'radical evil'. But I have given full reason, I trust, for holding that what is 'radical' cannot, *ipso facto*, be evil, and have shown that post-Kantian psychology, or at least the recent sciences of child-psychology and race psychology, render the assumption of any warp in our nature unnecessary and improbable, if not impossible. The hypothesis of a bias is purely gratuitous, and would never have presented itself, but for the dominion over men's minds of the doctrine of Original Right-

---

[1] F. R. Tennant, *Philosophical Theology* (1928), vol. 2, p. 258.
[2] Tennant, *The Origin and Propagation of Sin* (2 ed. 1908), Preface, pp. xxviii–xxix.

eousness . . . it is at least as legitimate to go out of our way in search
for a bias towards good, to explain cases where the moral sanction is
obeyed, as for a bias towards evil to explain cases where it is dis-
obeyed.[1]

In effect, Tennant refused to be impressed by the view which Karl Barth
was to revive, that sin was a mysterious intrusion into the divine plan. He
tried to draw a line between the traditional theological position that the
relationship between God and man was one of human rebellion, and the
view of some nineteenth-century German protestant theologians that sin
was an inevitable, or even necessary, part of human development.[2] According to his carefully restricted formula, 'the existence of moral evil would
seem to be the most easily justified to reverent speculation if it be looked
upon as the contingent product of a moral world, and not as having an
absolute purpose in the universe or in the self-manifestation of God'.[3] If
sin were the contingent product of a moral world, it was not an inexplicable
mystery, nor was it evidence of a 'massive disorder' in the universe, or of
a 'pathology' extending through the whole of existence.

Both these phrases occurred in a modern example of the continuing
traditional view of the relationship between God and man:

> Perhaps no one would deny that when we look at actual human
> existing, we perceive a massive disorder in existence, a pathology
> which seems to extend through all existence, whether we consider the
> individual or the community, and stultifies it. Because of this prevalent
> disorder, the potentialities of existence are not actualised as they might
> be, but are lost or stunted or distorted.[4]

The appeal from revelation to history did not dispose of Tennant's argument
against asserting the self-evidence of a 'bias towards evil'. In its High
Anglican context it was an appeal designed essentially to protect the
argument that because of the universality and solidarity of human disorder, there was within the human situation no remedy to hand that was
adequate, that only God, acting through Jesus, could redeem man from
his tragic destiny. Here, traditional theological propositions took precedence over any biologically-based interpretation of man's history, and
history itself was interpreted in monotone, as pathological.

After 1930, in fact, few writers pursued Tennant's effort to bring the two
disciplines together, Essays in the more empirical tradition appeared in
Biology and Personality (1965), a symposium edited by I. T. Ramsey, who
was both philosopher of religion and bishop of Durham, but the contributors
were chiefly concerned with problems like that of the status of human
personality in the light of brain operations. Only occasionally, as in J. A. T.
Robinson's study in christology, *The Human Face of God* (1973), did the

---

[1] Tennant, *The Origin and Propagation of Sin* (2 ed. 1908), Preface, pp. xxviii–xxix.
[2] For example, K. G. Bretschneider, *Dogmatics* (1838); Alexander Schweizer, *Christian Doctrine* (1877); H. Lüdemann, *Christian Dogmatics* (1926). Hegelian philosophy is more important than science in these writers.
[3] Tennant, *The Origin and Propagation of Sin* (2 ed. 1908), p. 137.
[4] J. Macquarrie, *Principles of Modern Theology* (1966), p. 59.

tension between mythology and biology come clearly out into the open. At an early stage of his argument Robinson said that in terms of modern biological knowledge the doctrine of the Virgin Birth had become meaningless: one could only properly speak of a 'man' if one meant someone born into the human evolutionary continuum, for being a man was given historically, within a temporal series of births; one could not just be 'as a man', but had to be a particular person, and this requirement was simply not met either by the classical idea of *anhypostasia*, according to which Christ was a divine person who assumed human nature without assuming human personality, or by the later modification of that position, *enhypostasia*, according to which the essence of humanity exists within the divinity of the Son, so that the human hypostasis or ego of Jesus had always existed within the Trinity. The 'divinity' of Jesus – which Robinson was prepared to affirm – did not depend on his being the incorporation of a heavenly figure from his birth. It depended on the quite different assumption that the Jesus-figure was being created by God from the beginning of the universe. There was no question of adoptianism: from his birth Jesus was the expression of the purpose of God. He was a man, Robinson said, who in all that he said and did as man was the personal representative of God. 'He stands in God's place, he *is* God to us and for us.'[1] But this capacity to represent God so fully that people naturally said of him that God was in him emerged in the process of evolution, within a series of temporal births. No discontinuity was involved, at either the natural or supernatural level. God raised Jesus up through the normal process of heredity and environment and made him his decisive word to men.

Up to this point Robinson had really been showing how readily specific scientific findings, like the data of biological evolution, can be integrated with a religious system: neither biology nor the doctrine of the divinity of Christ had suffered much so far. In the later part of the book, however, driven perhaps by his conviction that in an increasingly secularized western society men were not going to credit much longer a deity situated somehow outside his creation but intermittently intervening in it, Robinson tried, with the help of ideas drawn from Teilhard de Chardin, Dorothee Sölle[2] and (in the background) Hegel, to provide a workable myth of a god *inside* the creation. He turned to the myth of a human race which has to incarnate the World-Spirit. God is not yet immanent in our history because the race has not yet brought him fully into self-consciousness, and so he has to be represented. Jesus, Robinson said, was the sign of a new mutation in the world of Spirit, he was evidence of the reality of a coming new spiritual humanity in which all men would have a part, just as they had done in the order which linked them to the evolutionary past. Here, however, biology had become little more than the source of a handy metaphor ('mutation') which could be used to justify looking for discontinuity in the human future and so to bring back eschatology, the old Jewish hope that God would intervene in the present world-order and change the rules, with a slightly scientific air. And – partly because the conclusion was mediated by Hegel

[1] J. A. T. Robinson, *The Human Face of God* (1973), pp. 113–14.
[2] Dorothee Sölle, *Christ the Representative* (1967).

and Teilhard – one was not far from the vulgar progressivism which had flourished at the end of the nineteenth century.[1]

This free use of untestable myth was characteristic of one side of twentieth-century theology. This was true, for example, of Paul Tillich (1886–1974), whose *Systematic Theology* (2 vols 1951–57) was a restatement of Lutheranism in existentialist terms. In the 1920s (see p. 558) Tillich had hoped for a rapprochement between the German Protestant churches and the Social Democrats; driven out of Germany by the triumph of ecclesiastical conservatism and Nazi politics he went to the United States, where his theology became less revolutionary and his vocabulary much more Heideggerian.[2] The problems of 'Man' and society were shifted to a mythological level and attributed to man's tragic destiny, as fallen into a finite existence and incapable of 'authentic being'. 'Man as he exists is not what he essentially is', Tillich wrote, 'he is estranged from the ground of his being, from other beings, and from himself'.[3] Man might, according to Tillich, experience a finite freedom, but this freedom did not enable him to break out of his estrangement, but only to feel himself responsible for every act in which his estrangement was actualized. Sin and guilt were thus translated into the new idiom, and redemption followed, in the form of the 'new being' (Christ), a power from beyond man which healed his existential estrangement. In this pattern the underlying assumption, which had its antecedents in classical Christian theology, was that men and women as we encounter them are unable to be, and yet at the same time are responsible for not being, what their creator intended them to be. This was the assumption which Tennant wanted to drop, and which he argued was not somehow 'revealed' either in the book of Genesis, or in Paul's use of the Adam-story. Tillich, on the other hand, said that theology must represent the Fall, not as a story which happened once upon a time, but as a symbol of the universal human situation. Similarly, J. A. T. Robinson described the creation and fall stories as ways of giving theological expression to processes and experiences which were going on all the time. Robinson also applied this to the Parousia, which did not – he said – refer to a historical event in the future, but was part of a myth designed to clarify what was meant by seeing all things new in the Kingdom of God. 'It asserts that the reality depicted by the Fall, the truth of all things "in Adam", is not the only or final truth about the cosmic scene.'[4]

No doubt this approach, which is to be found in many other writers, is a means of saving traditional language from complete disuse – not many people talk about the Parousia, nowadays. But Tillich and Robinson seem

[1] Marxism and modern theology share an unwillingness to believe that human history is not moving towards an *end*. As Walter Benjamin wrote, thinking of the first half of the century, 'Social Democratic theory, and even more its practice, have been formed by a conception of progress which did not adhere to reality but made dogmatic claims' (*Illuminations*, 1970, p. 262).

[2] M. Heidegger (1889–1976) published *Being and Time* in 1927: 'what Heidegger did was to give philosophical seriousness, professorial respectability, to the love affair with unreason and death that dominated so many Germans in this hard time' – P. Gay, *Weimar Culture* (Penguin 1974),p. 85.

[3] P. Tillich, *Systematic Theology*, vol. 2, p. 51.

[4] J. A. T. Robinson, *The Human Face of God*, p. 117.

automatically to attribute truth to the myths which they select, as though, once they have decided to treat them as mythical instead of historical, their truth has been established. It is the truth-value of stories like the Fall-story which is in question, however. Of course the Parousia is a myth designed to interpret existence, but this gives no status to the attempt at interpretation. Nor can the Fall suddenly be taken for granted as a serious description of the position of mankind in the eyes of God *because* it no longer has to be, or can be, defended as historical event. In fact, if one drops the appeal to history in the case of the Fall, for example, one is left with a myth proper, similar to all other myths from China to Peru; as such, the myth becomes testable by experience in the present: a historical Fall was indisputable, a mythological Fall can be no more than an assertion, whose truth-value depends on its being able to give imaginative coherence to deeply-lodged human needs for meaning in existence. The myth no longer guarantees its own truth, one has to give grounds for supposing that in some sense the myth may point in the direction of reality. 'The conclusion one is driven to', wrote Van Harvey, the American theologian, 'is that the content of faith can as well be mediated through a historically false story *of a certain kind* as through a true one, through a myth as through history. Everything depends on the form and structure of the symbolism and the myth. But having said this, one must also say that the conditions of belief vary from age to age. What may have been intelligible to and valid for Augustine and Francis may not be so for those of us who live after the advent of biblical criticism.'[1] Myths, one might add, survive only as long as they can bear the destructive testing in time of human experience.

If one asks why Tillich (or Rudolf Bultmann, for example) should have turned to existentialism for assistance with theology, the answer is not to be found in the theology itself so much as in the reasons why existentialism gained ground among European intellectuals after 1920, and these reasons belong to the general history of western culture.[2] If one thinks of existentialism in this period as often the substitution of action for argument, of decision for cartesian doubt, Tillich's use of the approach was analogous to Karl Barth's more conventional fideism, and one senses a deeper continuity with Newman's growing horror, a century before, at the anti-dogmatism of the – as they seemed to him – rationalist liberals. But the attempt to lift the discussion onto another level, beyond the reach of rationalism if not necessarily of 'reason', was not always successful, because for many people by the beginning of the twentieth century the central theological problem had become: how much longer could the Christian religion maintain its claim to possess uniquely revealed, absolute religious truth? or should one now interpret Christianity as a stage in the spiritual development of one of humanity's larger cultural centres? Early nineteenth-century Hegelian theologians had objected to the implication of the classical doctrine of the Person of Christ, that the ideal man/god could be manifested in a single

---

[1] Van A. Harvey, *The Historian and the Believer* (1967), pp. 280–81.
[2] For trenchant criticism, see T. W. Adorno, *The Jargon of Authenticity* (Frankfurt, 1964, E.T. 1973).

historical existence; they dismissed such a view of the life of Jesus as an intolerable foreshortening of the historical process. Now, what had been put forward as philosophical speculation – the relativity of all historical religions and their tendency to converge upon an ultimate unity as yet unattained – was alleged as the inevitable consequence of an enlarged understanding of human history, religious as well as biological.

The best example of this trend was Tennant's German contemporary, Ernst Troeltsch (1865–1923), though Troeltsch was not a theologian in Tillich's or Barth's sense, but a historian of religion and a powerful philosopher of history: he was also influenced by his friend, Max Weber, the sociologist.[1] As a historian, Troeltsch rejected the classical theology which isolated Christianity from the rest of history on the basis of miracle – the incarnation and the resurrection, for example. He could see no ground for admitting a specifically Christian miraculous causality at these points, when Christian writers denied a similar miraculous causality to other world-religions which claimed miraculous events as part of their main tradition; and when Protestants, indeed, normally denied the reality of all Roman Catholic alleged miracles, and that on what were historicist grounds. Nor did he feel any inner religious need to grant as a faith-act (in the style which Karl Barth made familiar again in the 1920s) the extra-historical historicity of the incarnation and resurrection, events whose probability he had already criticized on the historical level. Christianity, as far as Troeltsch was concerned, was not to be limited to what could be defined in terms of these particular stories. Attacked by General Superintendent Kaftan of Kiel, Troeltsch said in the 1911 edition of *The Absoluteness of Christianity* that he did not mind the designation 'Christian Neoplatonist' bestowed on him by Kaftan and added: 'I comfort myself with the thought that God is not the General Superintendent of the universe and therefore continue unperturbably to regard myself as a Christian'.[2]

For Troeltsch, therefore, the uniqueness and absoluteness of Christianity could not be shown by an appeal to a supernatural divine revelation and incarnation. What could be shown was its historical individuality as the religious expression of a particular historical, western culture; but as Troeltsch also came to accept the individuality and self-sufficiency of the other great world-religions, this made it difficult for him to take the idealistic-evolutionary view, as he called it, that Christianity was absolute as the realization of the essence or idea of Religion itself. He did not believe that Hinduism, for example, had to seek its fulfilment in Christianity.

In his last lectures Troeltsch said that his study of the history of European civilization and of Christianity had led him to emphasize the historical individuality of both, and to attach much less significance to the idea of the supreme validity of either. Christianity's primary claim to any validity (not to *supreme* validity) was that only through Christianity had Europe become what it was, and that only in terms of it could Europe preserve the religious forces that were essential to its further development. He wrote:

[1] See especially E. Troeltsch, *The Absoluteness of Christianity* (1901, E.T. 1972). Also *Protestantism and Progress* (1912) and *Christian Thought* (1923).
[2] Troeltsch, *The Absoluteness of Christianity*, pp. 171–72.

We cannot live without a religion, yet the only religion that we can endure is Christianity, for Christianity has grown up with us and has become a part of our very being. Christianity could not be the religion of such a highly developed racial group if it did not possess a mighty spiritual power and truth; in short, if it were not, in some degree, a manifestation of the Divine Life itself. The evidence we have for this remains essentially the same, whatever may be our theory concerning absolute validity – it is the evidence of a profound inner experience. This experience is undoubtedly the criterion of its validity, but, be it noted, only of its validity for us. It is God's countenance as revealed to us . . . it is final and unconditional for us because we have nothing else . . . But this does not preclude the possibility that other racial groups, living under entirely different cultural conditions, may experience their contact with the Divine Life in quite a different way, and may also possess a religion which has grown up with them, and from which they cannot sever themselves as long as they remain what they are . . .[1]

Troeltsch applied his position logically to the case of Christian missions. Although missionary enterprise, he said, had always been in part simply a concomitant of the political, military and commercial enterprise of a state or nation, in part it was also an outcome of the religious enthusiast's passion for conversion. This latter aspect was directly connected with the claim of Christianity to possess absolute religious validity. Troeltsch distinguished between the (as he thought) crude religious systems of small tribes which were being morally and spiritually disintegrated by contact with western civilization, and which might be said to need the assistance of one of the so-called higher religions, and these great philosophical world-religions themselves. These non-Christian great religions had to be recognized as expressions of the general religious consciousness corresponding to certain definite types of culture, and it was their duty to increase in depth and purity by means of their own interior impulses, a task in which Christianity might assist them. But there should be no further question of thinking in terms of the conversion of the East, for example, to Christianity: a certain interpenetration of the great religious systems was all that was seriously conceivable.

Troeltsch died before the full secularizing effect of western culture on other societies had become apparent, and long before marxism had become the state-philosophy of China; his historical relativism was itself conditioned by the time at which he was writing; although he sometimes spoke as though Christianity might be replaced by another religious form, he usually assumed that the existing world-religions would survive through any foreseeable future; he also exaggerated the extent to which Christianity and western culture were bound together. Nevertheless, it was a pity that ideas of this kind did not develop more quickly out of the experience of missionary work in the nineteenth century: Christian missions in China, for instance, showed little appreciation of Chinese religion and culture in the nineteenth

[1] Troeltsch, *Christian Thought*, pp. 25–26.

century. When the Edinburgh Missionary Conference commission on the Christian message in relation to non-Christian religions reported in 1910 it admitted the 'wholly unnecessary alienation and misunderstanding which have thereby been created', but still spoke cheerfully, a few pages later, of 'the spectacle of the advance of the Christian Church along many lines of action to the conquest of the five great religions of the modern world'.[1]

The conclusion which Troeltsch reached, that the western Christian churches should give up the struggle to overthrow the non-Christian world-religions, represented the confluence of humanist ideas of toleration, philosophical and scientific ideas about development, the growth of a less dogmatic theological attitude (and the rapid general disappearance of belief in the moral standing of Hell), together with the all-pervasive effects of historical relativism. When one adds that Troeltsch expected the European religious tradition to move towards increasing individualism, one sees how unadapted to the immediate future were those religious factors which must have seemed, about 1914, most attuned to change. Racial and religious co-operation or interpenetration, toleration and individualism were not to be the obvious characteristics of the mid-twentieth century. Indeed, this synthesis of the legacy of the Enlightenment with Christian doctrine disintegrated overnight: after 1914 there came 'neo-orthodoxy'; a partial revival in some Protestant circles of the traditional authority of the Bible as the Word of God, an authority which the historical-critical method had seemed to have shattered for ever; of the classical Christian pessimism about human nature; and of the claim of Christianity to possess absolute religious truth, a claim which, as we have just seen, was virtually abandoned by theologians like Troeltsch who, nevertheless, did not want to abandon Christianity. The extent of the change becomes evident if one compares Troeltsch's views of the rôle of Christian missions with those of the Dutch theologian, Hendrik Kraemer (1890–1968), the most distinguished missionary theologian of the century.

Kraemer began, in terms which Troeltsch might have accepted, by rejecting the early nineteenth-century Protestant missionary assumption 'that this universe of living non-christian religions was adequately conceived by taking it to be a vast, degrading and decaying section of the spiritual life of mankind, steeped in darkness and error . . . The annals of modern missions testify to the natural vitality and tenacious strength as well as the inertia of these religions. They are the product of man's great efforts in the field of religion.'[2] Drawing on Karl Barth, not on Troeltsch, Kraemer extended this judgement to institutional Christianity itself, in as much as empirical, historical Christianity had also, he thought, to be understood as at least in part a specimen of human effort in the religious field. This human effort (and its *human* origin is the significant factor for Kraemer) produced various religious types – the naturalistic, the mystical, the moralistic and so forth – and these types of man's religious self-expression could be found in Christianity as well as in other religions.

---

[1] *World Missionary Conference 1910*, report of Commission iv, *The Missionary Message in relation to Non-Christian Religions*, p. 269, and p. 273.

[2] H. Kraemer, *The Christian Message in the Non-Christian World* (1938), pp. 284–85.

Man's religious consciousness, however, could not match the self-revelation of God in Christ: in historical Christianity what derived from man always led 'to the misapprehension of the prophetic religions of biblical realism'.[1]

In fact, although Kraemer sometimes referred to a general revelation, he deprived it of content. Even the Old Testament contained nothing more than a forward-looking glimpse of the revelation in Christ: Judaism itself was not a revealed religion. (There is a terrifying obtuseness in this readiness, in the 1920s and 1930s, to say that Judaism existed positively only to the extent that it served the interests of Christianity.) Christ was the one way of salvation, in him God became flesh, judged man, and made clear his purposes for man and the world. Kraemer spoke as though this revelation was an objective fact, independent of historical context or theological interpretation; he disclaimed any burden of proof – the burden lay on men themselves, who must surrender in faith to what stood before them objectively in Jesus. As for other religions, Kraemer judged them in terms of the norm given by God in Jesus Christ, and concluded that they were only the products of the human religious consciousness, in flight from God or in rebellion against him.

All this amounted to a familiar traditional theology, though now a provincial one. Faced with Troeltsch's acceptance of the historicity of all knowledge, Kraemer appealed to 'revelation', but could not show in what way its specific source, the Bible, was to be exempted from historicity and from the problems of language. At the meeting of the International Missionary Council in India in 1938 he exhorted the missionaries to witness to Christianity as the *truth*. He said that reluctance to convert or proselytise, the preference for social service or for a sharing of religious experience with people of other faiths as the only valid Christian missionary method, sprang from a fundamental confusion: conversion was the missionary duty.

> 'In the field of religion there was only one alternative. Either the paramount thing in a religion was that it contained objective truth, or its truth-quality was of secondary or even minor importance, and left one permanently trapped in relativism.'[2]

Whatever qualifications Kraemer might make, he was still defending the thesis of a radical discontinuity between Christianity and the other world-religions. Twenty years later the ecumenical leader, Visser't Hooft, described his book as a decisive factor in the turning away from a relativistic missionary ideology to a christocentric theology of missions. At a greater distance of time one may attribute Kraemer's success to missionary nostalgia for the theological certainties of a vanished era. Within a year of Tambaram the world war had begun, which was to bring about a marxist victory in China, and speed up the advance of the 'third world' to political independence of the West, and this foreshadowed the end of Christian missions in the sense in which Kraemer was still thinking about them in 1938. It was not surprising that by the 1960s more was heard of 'dialogue' than of 'discontinuity' in missionary circles. Nevertheless, the neo-orthodox

[1] *ib.* p. 285.
[2] *ib.* p. 296.

theological revival of which Kraemer formed a part characterized the years
between about 1920 and 1950. After the Second World War the sheer
complexity of the intellectual, moral and political problems facing
Christianity compelled the re-appearance of a more liberal theology, which
had for the moment despaired of 'revelation' and returned to 'reason' as the
source of religious truth. The principal difference between the 'radical
theology' of the 1960s and the 'liberalism' of the 1900s was that the old
optimistic philosophical idealism had less influence in the later period.

Kraemer's defence of the duty of Christianity to replace the other world-
religions in their own cultures, to do to them what it had failed in the long
run to do to Judaism, reflected the recovery of the more conservative point
of view from the 1890s. Throughout the nineteenth century, as has been
seen, two theological moods had conflicted: one, broadly optimistic, which
involved an acceptance that the structure of western society was changing
and would continue to change, and another, which might be called Christian
pessimist, which was often found associated with deep hostility to the
industrial, urban, technological and mass-democratic aspects of the modern
world. In the background lay the shock of the Russian revolution of 1917,
which seemed to embody all that the pessimists feared without producing
what the optimists wanted. Post-war chaos, the brief prosperity of the
1920s, the 1929 depression, set the background of a decade in which what
had seemed harmless ideologies, the quirks of irrelevant, eccentric men,
transformed themselves into political forces of terrifying efficiency: in the
1930s economic misery, Fascism, Nazism and Stalinism dominated men's
minds. To the extent that Russian marxism was officially anti-Christian,
and to the extent that the institutional churches had become permeated by
the collective hysteria of nationalism, which had its own anti-modernising
strain of violence, theological pessimism was strengthened. Theologians
reacted much as they had done to a similar psychological condition in the
early nineteenth century and reasserted the supernatural origin and
theological centrality of the ecclesia. One had to believe in the survival of
the Church in order to believe in Christianity, and the survival of the visible
Church seemed to require supernatural support: if the Church *was* the
Gospel, the Church was secure, and with the Church secured, there might
yet be time to save the Gospel.

This was part of the context of the ecumenical movement, the theological
drive for the unification of the Churches which is usually dated from the
World Missionary Conference which was held in Edinburgh in 1910. Part of
its causation was social: the mounting hostility of western society to
organized Christianity, the formation of competitive anti-Christian movements – Fascism, Marxism, Third World nationalism, the weakness of the
individual Churches as generators of the idea of God in human society – all
these factors pushed institutional Christianity towards organic unity of
some kind.[1] The theological discovery that the New Testament might be
said to favour this goal was hardly new; what was new was the willingness
of various Protestant bodies to devise, or try to devise solutions to the

[1] For the sociological view that the unity movement was a response to the weakness of
the individual churches concerned, see B. R. Wilson, *Religion in a Secular Society* (1966).

problems which the achievement of unity presented. In the past, when the Churches had thought of themselves as religious 'states', unity had been conceived either as the object of a kind of ecclesiastical imperialism, or perhaps as the outcome of a process of voluntary surrender by some Churches to others. In the 1930s and 1940s, however, the Protestant Churches seemed as though they might be about to break out of the fixed lines of the post-Reformation denominational system and to transcend this 'foreign policy' conception of the search for unity. Social change seemed to be making more fruitful negotiations possible, and theologians appeared to be able to rationalize the altered situation: the consequent theology, the work of committees rather than individuals, may be examined in the Reports of the long series of international conferences: Stockholm (1925), Lausanne (1927), Edinburgh and Oxford (1937), and Amsterdam (1948). Characteristic was the emphasis on the 'sins of our divisions'; on the certainty that Jesus's prayer that his followers might be one must be answered in terms of visible institutional and sacramental unity; and on episcopacy, with whatever necessary ambiguities of definition, as the basic structural form of the priesthood of the 'coming great Church', as it was sometimes called.

Theologically-speaking, however, the Protestant ecumenical movement had lost its momentum by the 1950s. Then in 1958 John XXIII was elected Pope and at the second Vatican Council in 1962 a new, essentially Roman Catholic ecumenical phase began, whose theological boundaries had not become completely clear by the 1970s. It looked, however, as though ecumenicity had slipped back into the 'diplomatic' forms of encounter, in which concepts like the papal primacy, Mariology, and the possession of valid ministerial orders were discussed with very traditional seriousness. Neither two centuries of Biblical criticism, nor our steadily accumulating knowledge of the history of institutional Christianity – whether in 'western' contexts or in 'overseas mission-fields', nor the growth of a highly sophisticated philosophical attitude to the use of words and myths in theology, had affected the confidence with which many ecumenical theologians handled such ideas. One example must be sufficient:

> The real presence of Christ's body and blood can, however, only be understood within the context of the redemptive activity whereby he gives himself, and in himself reconciliation, peace and life to his own. On the one hand, the eucharistic gift springs out of the paschal mystery of Christ's death and resurrection, in which God's saving purpose has already been definitively realised. On the other hand, its purpose is to transmit the life of the crucified and risen Christ to his body, the Church, so that its members may be more united with Christ and with one another.[1]

One could expound such sentences on the ground that they involved a specifically Christian mythological use of language, and that a Christian had as much right to arrange experience in *his* way as a marxist had to

[1] *An Agreed Statement on Eucharistic Doctrine* (1971 republished, unaltered 1973), iii.6. This was a Roman Catholic-Anglican statement.

arrange experience in *his* way; but such an argument, which took a plurality
of doctrinal positions for granted, was alien to the convictions of those who
made doctrinal statements like these. In the ecumenical world, on its post-
Vatican II basis, the united ecclesia, the coming great Church, was its own,
essentially supernatural authority, and could sanction the traditional
dogmatic system which liberalism had abandoned in despair. It looked
clear in the 1970s that organic unity would be achieved by moving closer
to the Roman Catholic system.

Again, only one example can be given: in this case the movement
towards a consensus on the doctrine of the eucharist. This emerged in a
remarkable series of documents: *A Lutheran-Roman Catholic Statement: the
Eucharist as Sacrifice* (St. Louis, Missouri, 1967); *The Eucharist in Ecumenical Thought*, a World Council of Churches paper finally agreed at
Louvain in 1971; the Anglican-Roman Catholic *Agreed Statement on Eucharistic Doctrine* (1971); and a statement worked out by French Reformed and
French Roman Catholic theologians, usually referred to as the *Les Dombes*
statement (1972).

These documents proposed a common understanding of the idea of the
presence of Christ in the eucharist. To quote the *Agreed Statement*:

> Communion with Christ in the Eucharist presupposes his true presence
> effectually signified by the bread and wine which, in this mystery,
> become his body and blood . . . the elements are not mere signs;
> Christ's body and blood become really present and are really given.
> But they are really present and given in order that, receiving them,
> believers may be united in communion with Christ the Lord.[1]

A footnote on the word 'transubstantiation' made the approach clear:

> The word is commonly used in the Roman Catholic Church to indicate
> that God acting in the eucharist effects a change in the inner reality of
> the elements. The term should be seen as affirming the *fact* of Christ's
> presence and of the mysterious and radical change which takes place.
> In contemporary Roman Catholic theology it is not understood as
> explaining *how* the change takes place.[2]

There was nothing very new theologically in this quiet dropping of the
Aristotelian pilot, or in the way in which the word 'fact' was introduced
into the passage: the roots of the consensus ran back to *The Fulness of
Sacrifice* (1930) by F. C. N. Hicks, and to *The Christian Sacrifice* (1932) by
E. Masure. These documents might be said to show that liberal theology,
in the best meaning of the words, had never finally established itself
ecclesiastically, however prominent individual liberal theologians might
have been. It was not clear whether the *Agreed Statement*, for example, was
intended to rule out Receptionism (or Virtualism) altogether as alternative
positions, but it was clear enough that only one doctrinal interpretation of
the rite was mentioned. The authors of the statement said that they
intended to reach a consensus on the level of faith, so that all might be able

[1] *Modern Eucharistic Agreement* (1973), pp. 28–29.
[2] *ib.*

to say, within the limits of the document itself, 'this is the christian faith of the eucharist'. This implied that if one did not agree with the view expressed there, that in the eucharistic rite the bread and wine *become* (the word was used frequently) the body and blood of Christ, one was rejecting part, at least, of the Christian faith of the eucharist. To some this might seem obviously true; to others, however, it might well seem a rejection of the idea of a plurality of doctrinal interpretation, an idea which is fundamental to any 'liberal' sharing in the eucharistic rite, and also to the liberal theological position as such.

In Protestant circles the dominant figure in conservative academic theology was that of Karl Barth (1886–1968). Barth reacted against the whole cultural situation in which Liberal Protestantism existed only as a minor theme; he wanted Christianity to cut itself free, not just from the anthropocentricism and historical relativism which he felt had corrupted German religious thought from Schleiermacher to Troeltsch, but from every positive trend in western culture. This is the point at which to recall his most striking contribution to twentieth-century theology, his *Commentary* on the Epistle to the Romans, first published in 1918, much altered in the second edition of 1921. This edition was not subsequently changed, but short prefaces revealed the author's reaction to criticism; the sixth edition was translated into English by Sir Edwyn Hoskins in 1933, by which time the sharpness of the original was already blunted by events. The later *Church Dogmatics*, begun in 1932 and left unfinished at his death, was broadly anticipated in the Romans Commentary, but the desire to make the dogmatic system totally christocentric over-indulged Barth's taste for speculative theology, and explained why Dietrich Bonhoeffer thought that Barth had lost sight of the importance of the Word as God's intention to communicate with men. If Troeltsch saw the absoluteness of the Christian revelation dissolving in the haze of historical relativism, Barth's primary vision was of a revelation so absolute that it reduced everything human to a common level of helpless inadequacy or wilful rebellion. Given the total adequacy of God, however, Barth in his later years defended the idea of universal salvation.

This attitude was the strength and weakness of Barth's position. In a sense he simply turned Feuerbach, whose analysis of the origin of religious he thought especially penetrating, against himself. He agreed that all historical religion, much of what passed for Christianity included, was a product of the human spirit alone, but whereas Feuerbach had said that western man projected as his idea of God a noble idealization of man, Barth argued that human ideas of God, precisely because they *were* human, were distortions which led away from God himself. This was the root of the trouble in his debates in the 1920s with von Harnack, who saw no virtue in rejecting natural theology as a genuine source of knowledge about God. But for Barth only God himself could reveal himself, and he had done so only once, in Jesus Christ, the Word of the Father who became flesh for our salvation, and returned to the Father, to be present for ever in the Church through the Holy Spirit. This revelation, moreover, was recorded once and for all in the Bible. Logically, man, unable to look into himself for truth, could not expect to be able to read the truth about God for himself in the Bible; he had to depend on the working of the Holy Spirit to reveal Christ to him as the Word within the Scriptures. Scripture had to 'become' the Word of God, and Barth used this as a way of distinguishing between himself and the 'fundamentalist' theologians who, he thought, treated the Bible as a thing instead of an event, relying too much on the words and not enough on the Word. Barth, that is, tested everything by what he regarded as the Reformation understanding of the idea of justi- fication by grace; at the same time he reaffirmed one important difference between Protestantism and Roman Catholicism, which, as recently as the First Vatican Council, had restated the medieval belief that reason was more than a sinfully distorted instrument.

Barth's brilliant writing could not always conceal the weakness of his theological method, which left him with only one argument, the appeal to the Bible as the one divine revelation. Human creativity had always to be pinned down as necessarily a source of error in theology; Kierkegaard, for example, at first seized on as a nineteenth-century fore-runner, was finally dismissed as an anthropocentric theologian. The absoluteness of the method helps to explain the opaqueness of his treatment of Schleiermacher in *Protestant Thought in the Nineteenth Century* (1952, E.T. 1972, chapter 13): to make any concessions to what Schleiermacher was actually trying to do would have meant admitting that his predecessor, schooled in such writers as Lessing and Semler, had foreseen the troubles which would come to a Protestant theology which staked everything on an appeal to the Jewish- Christian writings as the unique self-revelation of God. It was a logical corollary of his commitment to this view of revelation that Barth should be obliged to give up the traditional doctrine of analogy (*analogia entis*), which implied that some kind of being was common to God and man, so that man did not depend entirely on divine revelation for his knowledge of God but could argue, for example, from what he knew of ordinary human love to the idea of love as it might be found in God, and to substitute the analogy of grace (*analogia gratiae*), according to which it was only because God had first revealed to us the nature of divine love (or fatherhood, or personality) that man was able to understand human love or fatherhood. (One is reminded of the way in which most Victorian missionaries took it for granted that what they believed to be the 'christian' idea of marriage must become the accepted form of marriage in every culture which they en- countered.) The idea was dramatic rather than intelligible. (For a brilliant discussion of the subject, see *Analogy*, by H. Palmer, 1973.) Barth, in his study of Anselm, *Fides Quaerens Intellectum* (1930), insisted that man made no existential contribution to his own enlightenment at that point; there was no 'leap of faith' in his later revelational theology. Once a divinely and miraculously given 'faith' had taken over, human reason could understand what it was given to understand by and about God.

Barth's rejection of the critical or liberal style in theology was total: such thinkers had chosen the wrong place to start, and this invalidated what they said. This helps to explain the unfairness of the judgment which put Schleiermacher among the 'particular fathers' of the theological errors whose final phase was the 'German-Christian' movement which welcomed Nazism in the early 1930s. 'The doctrinal attitude of the German-Christians', Barth wrote in 1933, 'is nothing but a particular result of the entire neo-protestant development since 1700'.[1] In its historical context one follows the generalization, but it was the behaviour of the whole of German Protestant-ism since 1789, not just one part of it, that was on trial between 1918 and 1945. Perhaps in that confused situation Barth's gift was that of the preacher rather than the theologian – he excelled in the kind of language which reawakened men's belief in the relevance of a transcendent, omni-potent and righteous God who chose to reveal himself in Christ and justified men by grace alone. This may be illustrated by a passage on the resurrection of Christ:

> The resurrection is not a historical event which may be placed side by side with other events. Rather it is the 'non-historical' happening by which all other events are bounded, and to which events before and on and after Easter Day point . . . Were there a direct and causal con-nexion between the historical 'facts' of the resurrection – the empty tomb, for example, or the appearances detailed in 1 Cor 15 – and the resurrection itself; were it in any sense a 'fact' in history, then no profession of faith or refinement of devotion could prevent it being in the see-saw of 'Yes' and 'No', life and death, God and man, which is characteristic of all that happens on the historical plane . . . The con-ception of the resurrection, however, wholly forbids this method of procedure: why seek ye the living among the dead? The conception of the resurrection emerges with the conception of death and with the conception of the end of all historical things as such.[2]

This was the younger, paradoxical and perhaps more convincing Barth who was prepared to assert that just because the resurrection-stories of the New Testament offered problems to the historian, *belief* in the resurrection offered no problems at all: one had simply to grasp that the 'resurrection' was a 'non-historical' event with which 'appearances' and the 'empty tomb' had no essential link, that this was a spiritual disclosure and apprehension of God in Jesus.

Years later, however, in *Church Dogmatics*, Barth, perhaps now less willing to balance Christ against the Scriptures in a manner worthy of Luther, so altered his language as to convince many of his critics that he was now affirming the historicity of the resurrection after all. 'It is sheer superstition', he said, 'to suppose that only things which are open to 'historical' verification can have happened in time. There may have been events which happened far more really in time than the kind of things which Bultmann's scientific historian can prove. There are good grounds for supposing that the history of the resurrection of Jesus is a pre-eminent instance of such an event.'[3] Looked at more closely, however, his later

[1] K. Barth, *The German Church Conflict*, ed. T. H. L. Parker (1965), p. 16; the judgement on Schleiermacher is on p. 27.

[2] K. Barth, *The Epistle to the Romans*, tr. E. C. Hoskyns, 1933, pp. 203–205.

[3] K. Barth, *Church Dogmatics* (ET 1960), III/2, p. 446.

statements still seem to depend on the very unsatisfactory category of 'non-historical history'. The difference between the earlier and later versions seems to be that whereas in the commentary on *Romans* Barth used a very vague description of the resurrection (while vigorously asserting its status as non-historical history), in *Church Dogmatics*, on the other hand, the description of the resurrection became much more traditional, with the *bodily* nature of the 'appearances' and the story of the empty tomb now firmly in the foreground. He did not answer the questions which the historical critic raises about these narratives, however, but asserted that they described an event beyond the reach of historical research or description. This amounts to saying that the appearances of Jesus had a 'non-physical physicality', and that the state of the tomb was that of a 'non-empty emptiness'. Paradox breaks down when it is pushed so far. As Van Harvey commented, on the one hand Barth appealed to the seeing and hearing of the risen Jesus by the disciples as though it were a matter of the employment of common-sense categories like sight and hearing; on the other hand, he immunized the stories against assessment by saying that they were not literal or historical.[1]

Barth believed – and here he was at the very root of the problem of the modern theologian – that the Bible was the sum total of the sources in terms of which Christianity could be defined. Human religious experience, and human reflection on that experience, became irrelevant if one wanted to decide what God had revealed in Jesus Christ. Traditional literalism had lost its authority, however, and so Barth constantly invented categories which would express his Coleridgian conviction that the unique Word of God was in the Bible. A good example of this was his treatment, in *Church Dogmatics*, of the biblical doctrine of creation. The statement that God created the heaven and earth and man could not, he said, be advanced on any sort of human ground. The impregnable basis of this fact was that it was in the Bible, in the twofold creation narrative in *Genesis*, and in later recollection and comment on them in the Bible itself. These narratives should not be accepted as self-authenticating in some human fashion, however, but had to be understood through Christ. Thus Barth established his *credo ut intelligam*: I believe in Jesus Christ in order to understand that God created the heaven and the earth, and if I did not understand the former I could not understand the latter.

Nevertheless, the status of the creation stories had still to be established: how, if they were 'historical', could they have been recorded? Barth introduced a distinction between what he called 'saga' and 'myth', defining saga as an intuitive and poetic picture of a pre-historical reality of history which had been enacted once and for all in time and space. The creation stories were pure saga, and therefore worked on the divine level, whereas myth worked only on the level of human experience and explanation. Only the Holy Spirit, of course, could guide the faithful reader into knowing which parts of the Bible were saga and which were myth. The content of saga was, inevitably, 'non-historical history', which was now called the soul of history in the ordinary sense. The authors of the biblical sagas were

[1] Van A. Harvey, *The Historian and the Believer* (1967), p. 159.

summoned, claimed and committed to exploit the possibilities of historical
divination and poetry, and to make himself explicit Barth said that the
authors had been encountered by God. Yet his use of the phrase 'intuitive
and poetic' suggested that he was aware of the weakness of his own
argument in his own terms – that he was attributing divine creative power
to the human imagination, and he fell back rather lamely on the assertion
that in the last resort one had to receive and accept the witness of the Bible
through the power of the Holy Spirit. This was what Dietrich Bonhoeffer
meant when he spoke, in *Letters and Papers from Prison* (E.T. 1967, p. 152),
of Barth's 'positivism of revelation', his take-it-or-leave-it-position. Barth,
moreover, had left himself without any objective means of distinguishing
between Christian miracles and non-Christian miracles, or Christian sacred
writings and non-Christian sacred writings, though in both the non-
Christian cases he was obliged to deny any question of a divine revelation,
in act or word.[1]

Finally, the strength and weakness of Barth's theology become obvious
if one examines his exposition of the doctrine of the work of Christ in
Church Dogmatics, 11/1, *The Doctrine of God* (E.T. 1957). Barth intended
this version of the doctrine to be pauline. Expounding *Phillipians* 2.6 he
wrote that Christ 'shared in the status, constitution and situation of man
in which man resists God and cannot stand before him but must die. How
could God resist himself? How could God sin? The Son of God knew no sin.
But he could enter into man's mode of being, being in the flesh, in which
there is absolutely no justification before God (Romans 3.20) but only sin.
God could – and not only could but did – allow his Son to be in the flesh,
and therefore make him to be sin for our sakes, to become the object which
must be the object of his own anger' (pp. 397–98). In a powerful attempt to
explain how God could stage this internal interplay of mercy and righteousness Barth said that our criticism of God's justice was fundamentally a
failure to recognize our own sinfulness. He continued:

> In a complete resignation not of the essence but the form of his god-
> head (Christ), took upon himself our own human form . . . he stepped
> into the heart of the inevitable conflict between the faithfulness of God
> and the unfaithfulness of man . . . He was not only the God who is
> offended by man. He was also the man whom God threatens with
> death, who falls a victim to death in face of God's judgement[2].

The strength lay in the coolness with which Barth stated the unknowable.
The weakness came out in the final contrast: 'he was not only the God who
is *offended* by man, he was also the man whom *God* threatens with death.'
In his perpetual anxiety to safeguard the primacy of God Barth made him
the major partner in the second clause as well as in the first. Whereas, if the
balance which is inherent in the (admittedly obscure) concept of incarnation
were to be preserved, one would have expected something like: 'he was also

[1] K. Barth, *Church Dogmatics* (ET 1959), 111/2: the argument is taken from pp. 1–93;
the definition of saga is on p. 81.

[2] K. Barth, *Church Dogmatics* (ET 1957), 11/1, p. 397.

the man who makes his case against God's wrath'. Of course, Barth could
not say this. He had even written, earlier in the same passage, that 'he
(Christ) and not Israel is the one who really suffers in all that the Jews of
today have to endure',[1] a comment which summed up the whole of Jürgen
Moltmann's later discussion of Auschwitz in *The Crucified God* (E.T. 1974),
but which pushed the idea of substitution beyond any serious intellectual
or moral reality. Barth eschewed the liberal tradition, from Schleiermacher
through Jowett to Tennant, too completely; he did not remember that – as
Tennant, for example, would certainly have insisted – no theological
method is trustworthy which obliterates men and women so entirely. A
generation even before Schleiermacher, J. G. von Herder, a humanist-
Christian in the German Enlightenment, had warned that there must be no
Favoritvolk: 'the negro is as much entitled to think the white man degenerate as the white man to think the former a black beast'.[2] He rejected
colonialism, whether military or missionary. A historical relativist, he
valued the individual creativity of seemingly incommensurable cultures,
and he did not suppose that God would prove less discriminating. *Mutatis
mutandis*, Troeltsch was to say much the same thing, but in general the
lesson had been lost as Europe moved through industrial expansion to the
racialism, militarism and social inhumanity of the late nineteenth century.
Barth believed that he had a mission to protest against a Christian humanism – which he often identified as 'neo-protestantism' – which was secularizing the Christian religion. He misunderstood his period: it was not from
excessive humanism, whether Christian or otherwise, that the first half of
the twentieth century suffered.

   Those who thought – as Barth did, and as others still do – that Liberal
Protestantism was the natural religious expression of every anthropocentric
tendency in western culture, and who, somewhat perversely, also blamed
Liberal Protestantism for the failure of Roman Catholic as well as Protestant
orthodoxy to prevent the rise of the great totalitarian political movements,
and for whom, in the second half of the century, 'Communism' remained
the principal enemy, were horrified by the quiet academic recovery of
liberal theology in the 1960s, when the influence of Bultmann, Tillich, and
a rediscovered and partially misinterpreted Dietrich Bonhoeffer (1906–45)
began to counter-balance that of Barth and the neo-orthodox, ecumenical
movement. Yet this was hardly a revival of the philosophically naive,
socially optimistic, science-orientated liberalism of the Edwardian period
at its worst, as in *Liberal Christianity* (E.T. 1903) by the French theologian
Jean Réville (1854–1907), or, with Hegelian overtones, *The New Theology*
(1907), the product of a brief flirtation with radicalism by R. J. Campbell
(1867–1956). The liberalism of the 1960s was much more a liberalism of
desperation. Earlier liberals had usually assumed that some kind of
'modernisation' was the key to a general renewal of Christian belief, but
their successors increasingly thought of critical theologies as the safeguard
of a minority, not the watchword of a majority. This explains the popularity
of Bonhoeffer's posthumously published *Letters and Papers from Prison*

---

[1] *ib.* p. 395.
[2] See I. Berlin, *Vico and Herder* (1976), p. 198.

(E.T. 1955). For although he saw the problem too much as one of communication (the theory that the problem was how to translate the known and unchanging gospel into 'modern' terms), at least Bonhoeffer started from the assumption (which the later liberals shared) that western culture was moving towards what would be a completely non-Christian phase; and when he asked himself the relevant question, how was one to speak of Christianity in a society which had no shared Christian or other religious assumptions, he did not suppose that either Barth's biblicism, or existentialism in the manner of Bultmann and Tillich, would provide an answer. Troeltsch had thought that western culture and western Christianity were indissolubly bound together, but Bonhoeffer thought that the links were dissolving, and he grasped something of the predicament of a religion without a culture, unable (unlike the Church in the European Dark Ages) to impose itself on the new environment. Barth, in as far as he had understood what was happening, had chosen to believe that this stateless and cultureless condition was the natural form of Christianity – this was the root of his political and ecclesiological views, and this was the point at which he and Bonhoeffer stood in profound agreement, over against all those who now disinterred various kinds of panentheism, progressivism, Hegelianism, 'christian-marxism' and so forth, in order to be able to declare that despite appearances, western culture would not and could not enter a non-religious phase.[1] Bonhoeffer dismissed Tillich, for example, as setting out to interpret the evolution of the world, *against its will*, in a religious sense. Nevertheless, Bonhoeffer disagreed with Barth's acceptance of a kind of extra-territorial status for the ecclesia: instead, he thought that the followers of Jesus had to struggle back into the secular culture, but that they could do this only by reinterpreting their biblical concepts from inside it. Because of his tragic death, his ideas remained obscure at this point, but he seems to have thought that the alternative to (a) theological development, which was proving as untenable as other ideas of historical continuity, and to (b) a pure eschatological theology which tried to behave as though religious ideas were changeless and had no cultural existence at all, was a theology of historical adaptation, in which one pole would be the 'lordship' of Jesus over all cultures conceivable, and the other the actual historical environment, which obeyed neither a secular marxist necessity nor the hidden hand of divine providence. Two problems followed. First, how to fill out, in theory or in experience, the idea of the Lordship of Christ; and second, that at a time when change was self-conscious and continual, the concept of a particular and definable historical environment seemed to recede indefinitely.

This illustrated the way in which liberal theology always seemed to come back to the same difficulties. His anti-dogmatic programme, part moral in origin, part philosophical, threw the liberal theologian back on the New Testament and on the personality and teaching (rather than Person and

---

[1] Theologians like the American Charles Hartshorne (b. 1897), and the British L. S. Thornton (1884–1960), who made use of the work of scientific philosophers like A. N. Whitehead (1861–1947); Tillich and Teilhard de Chardin, and their popularizers, are other instances.

Work) of Jesus. At the same time, however, his historical method, which was based on questions of probability in terms of evidence, and not on an *a priori* rejection of miracle as the neo-orthodox often misleadingly asserted, made the New Testament version of the teaching of Jesus less authoritative and the historical personality less acceptable. From the early nineteenth century onwards, therefore, the liberal theologian turned for assistance to religious experience, hoping, as Schleiermacher already clearly hoped, that the religious experience of the individual in the ecclesia would confirm that both Christian dogma, and the Christian tradition about the Person of Jesus, were inherently part of the conceptual and psychological structure of the ordinary human being.

It was in this way that Bultmann's demythologizing approach to the New Testament could be regarded as radical. One went *behind* the biblical myths, announcing not only what they had meant in the past, but also their alleged meaning in the present experience of a Lutheran-type Christian. Bultmann, like Tillich, crossed from the biblical myths to contemporary, more especially western experience through existential philosophy (especially that of Heidegger). Bultmann tried to bring justification by faith and existentialism together by describing salvation as a present, self-authenticating experience of deliverance from existence as an intolerable burden of suffering, guilt and the fear of death – what Heidegger called 'inauthentic existence'. Religious revelation was not a divine communication of knowledge, propositions to be believed, but an event (the life, death and resurrection of Jesus) taking place here and now, which abolished death and put the man who accepted faith into a new situation – authentic existence in Heidegger's language, Tillich's 'new being'. Exactly how Bultmann and Tillich related this secular existential experience of the mystery of being to the Christian symbolic system was never altogether clear, but Bultmann, for example, said that divine revelation did not present men with an objective world-view; indeed, world views were useless, because they led a man away from the self-understanding that he needed. Nor was revelation a matter of asserting that certain historical events happened in the past, or that one should believe certain extraordinary dogmatic statements. Rather the man of faith grasped the self-understanding which was divinely offered him in his existential present so that he understood himself, not only as one who came from a sinful past and stood under God's judgment, but also as one who was freed from this past by the divine grace which encountered him in the world.[1]

At this stage Bultmann moved back to a conservative, partially Lutheran position. Human experience, he claimed, at any rate as contained in twentieth-century existential philosophy of some kinds, offered a self-understanding which might be seen as a secular version of Pauline and Johannine anthropology. (Since Bultmann denied that revelation consisted of a world-view, he could not, of course, claim that this anthropology had absolute value.) This philosophical discovery, however, gave no positive standing either to humanism or to other religious systems, for, Bultmann

---

[1] R. Bultmann, *Existence and Faith* (ET 1964), p. 101. From 'The Concept of Revelation in the New Testament' (1929).

said, it was only the prior act of God in the Christ-event which made men capable of faith, love and authentic human existence. How this happened Bultmann could not say, except that the Christ-event negated human self-assertion and human values, a view rather like that on which Albert Schweitzer fell back at the end of the *Quest of the Historical Jesus*. Out of this negation, presumably, one passed into faith.

The success of Bultmann's argument obviously depended on confining the discussion of the religious consciousness and its secular analogue to western Christian and philosophical sources, but there was no reason why writers from other traditions should accept this limitation. Moreover, if one appeals to the existential result – to the Christ-event as the one possible source of authentic human being – one is appealing to the evidence of the human self-consciousness in historical time. Twentieth-century Christian theologians still make this claim about the transforming effect of the Christ-event on human nature with extraordinary confidence. Non-Christian cultures, however, which by now have considerable experience of the western world, would not necessarily agree with the flattering view which the west – in Bultmann, for example – took of Christianity as deliverance to faith, love and authentic human existence; they might prefer the kind of human being moulded in other religious traditions; they might equally argue that these same non-Christian traditions produced 'authentic human existence' quite as often as did the western religious tradition itself. Few modern Christian theologians, however liberal they may deem themselves to be, take seriously enough the attitude expressed in Herder's aphorism, that the negro is as much entitled to think the white man degenerate as the white man to think the former a black beast. And like all theologians Bultmann tended to exaggerate the finality of his interpretation of the New Testament gospels; it was arguable, for instance, that Jesus, as far as the traditions about him are reliable, spoke more of divine forgiveness than he did about a divine transformation of human nature; Luther himself was perhaps a safer guide than Bultmann at this point.

For the liberal theologians, then, the appeal to the Spirit of Jesus led to the problems of history; the appeal to 'myth', or 'the poetic use of language' ended in comparative literature; the appeal to the religious consciousness ended in the problem of the relationship between Christianity and other faiths. In the last case, the logical conclusion may be found in a book like *God and the Universe of Faiths* (1973) by John Hick, for whom Christianity was one of a group of world faiths, each of which provided the principal path of salvation for a large section of the human race. He argued that the view that Jesus proclaimed himself to be God incarnate, and to be the one point of saving contact between God and man, lacked adequate historical foundation. The fact – which he accepted – that Christians experienced salvation through Christ did not mean that salvation could not be experienced in any other way. 'The alternative possibility is that the ultimate divine reality – in our Christian terms, God – has always been pressing in upon the human spirit, but always in ways which leave men free to open or close themselves to the divine presence.'[1] He used the phrase, 'the universe

[1] J. Hick, *God and the Universe of Faiths* (1973), p. 145.

of faiths', to express the hypothesis that at their experiential roots all the great religious systems came into contact with the same ultimate reality. He also spoke of 'the Copernican revolution in theology', by which he meant that there was taking place a shift from the dogma that Christianity was at the centre of the theological universe to the realization that God must be thought of as the centre, while all the religions of mankind, including the western Christian religion, serve and revolve around him. This was language not unlike Troeltsch's, but strengthened by the fact that it was spoken in a post-colonial and not an imperialistic period as far as the west was concerned: a post-colonial west needs a post-colonial theology.

How, then, did the state of theology appear in the 1970s? Orthodoxy and critical liberalism had, not for the first time, reached a potential point of parting. Karl Rahner, as a senior Roman Catholic theologian, and the kind of German Protestant thinking associated with such men as Gerhard Ebeling, Jurgen Moltmann and Wolfhart Pannenberg, represented continuing orthodoxies which still took for granted the essential truth of such dogmas as: the divinity as well as the humanity of Christ; the need for a supernatural, self-sacrificing mediator to restore an allegedly broken fellowship between created and creator; the supernatural origin of the Church; the necessity of at least two sacraments, in one of which it may be said that the elements *become* the body and blood of Jesus Christ. Propositions of this kind are regarded in practice as knowledge, in the sense that they can be *taught* (in schools, for example), not just discussed. Movements in art, philosophy and science, not to speak of social change, have not substantially modified these positions since 1800, though they have modified the way in which individual orthodox theologians present them. The mainstream churches have neither modified the historic creeds since 1800, nor changed their liturgical significance. At the wider level of practising religious communities orthodoxy spills over into movements like pentecostalism, which have more psychological and social interest than theological value. The debate about secularization, which has gone on intensely in sociological circles since 1945, was really about the extent to which this general orthodoxy had ceased (or continued) to provide the mental framework through which ordinary men and women in the west interpreted the broader meanings of their life-experience. (The best modern discussion of the subject was in *The Secularisation of the European Mind in the Nineteenth Century*, 1975, by Owen Chadwick.)

Critical liberalism certainly failed, between 1800 and the 1970s, to replace the varieties of orthodoxy as far as the mainstream churches were concerned. This was perhaps because statements of the critical position, *The Remaking of Christian Doctrine* (1974) by Maurice Wiles, for example, inevitably seemed parasitic on the kind of orthodox propositions which have just been mentioned. Liberal theologians were committed, as long as they wanted to remain theologians in the Christian tradition, to the belief that western religious thought and behaviour must stem from the Bible and the Church in history, whatever other sources were drawn on in addition. They were like politicians who perpetually proposed legislative changes which somehow never reached the statute-book. On questions of ethics, especially sexual ethics, theological liberals had powerful social support which helped them, as in the case of the Anglican Church's volte-face on contraception, to obtain important results. But pure theology had only an ecclesiastical environment, it had no other social roots by the 1970s. Those outside the Churches were no longer interested in the liberal theologian's desire to qualify rather than replace what the Churches officially said in the realm of pure theology. They made little of the difference between saying that Christ was divine, and saying that it was supremely through Jesus that God's purposes and the experience of grace had been made effective in the world. Liberalism was available to the individual, but it was not available to the institution. And so a certain split had taken place. Certain kinds of religious behaviour belonged to and took place within the environment of the Churches; certain styles of religious thinking had for the moment ceased to belong to the environment of the Churches. J. S. Bezzant diagnosed this situation accurately some years ago:

> I think it is entirely reasonable for any man who studies the spirit of the facing of life as Christ faced it, and his recorded teaching, to decide that by him he will stand through life, death or eternity rather than join in a possible triumph of evil over him. Whether or not any Church will regard such a man as a Christian is nowadays wholly secondary and manifestly relatively unimportant.[1]

[1] J. S. Bezzant, in *Objections to Christian Belief* (1963), pp. 109–110.

Suggested Reading

A serious course of reading in *modern* theology should probably begin with Kant's *Religion Within the Limits of Reason Alone* (Harper Torchbooks, New York 1960), and H. S. Reimarus, *Fragments* (ed C. H. Talbert, SCM Press 1971). Of nineteenth-century theology, S. Kierkegaard's *Last Years* (Collins 1965), J. H. Newman's *The Grammar of Assent* (1870), Matthew Arnold's *Literature and Dogma* (1873), and Charles Darwin's *The Descent of Man* ([2]1874), all throw light on the growth of the modern religious situation. F. Nietzsche's *Twilight of the Idols* and *The AntiChrist* (Penguin 1969) and *Beyond Good and Evil* (Penguin 1973), remain indispensable for any understanding of the modern world. My last strictly Victorian choice would be William James, *The Will to Believe* (1897).

In the twentieth century any list of primary texts should include, for example: E. Troeltsch, *The Absoluteness of Christianity* (SCM Press 1972); F. von Hügel, *The Mystical Element in Religion* (1890); Karl Barth, *The Epistle to the Romans* (OUP 1968); M. Heidegger, *Being and Time* (SCM Press 1962; Blackwell paperback 1979); N. Berdyaev, *The Meaning of History* (Bles 1936), and *Solitude and Society* (Bles 1938); R. Bultmann, *Existence and Faith* (Fontana 1973); D. Bonhoeffer, *Letters and Papers from Prison* (The Enlarged Edition, SCM Press 1971); and Simone Weil, *Gravity and Grace* (Routledge Kegan Paul 1972); W. Pannenberg, *Basic Questions in Theology* (3 vols, SCM Press 1970–72); Dorothee Sölle, *Suffering* (Darton, Longman and Todd 1975).

The tension, rather than development, in modern Catholic theology, might be represented by: M. Blondel, *Letter on Apologetic and History and Dogma* (Harvill 1964); G. Daly, *Transcendence and Immanence, a Study in Catholic Modernism* (OUP 1980); G. Tyrrell, *Christianity at the Cross-Roads* (1909); B. M. G. Reardon, *Catholic Modernism* (a reader, A. & C. Black 1970) A. Flannery (ed), *Vatican Council II* (documents, Costello Publishing Company 1975); C. Butler, *The Theology of Vatican II* (Darton Longman and Todd [2]1981); K. Rahner, *Theological Investigations* (vols 1–17, Darton Longman and Todd 1965–81); H. Küng, *Infallible?* (Fontana 1971) and *The Church – Maintained in Truth* (SCM Press 1980); E. Schillebeeckx, *Christ: The Christian Experience in the Modern World* (SCM Press 1980).

Useful general introductions are: S. Ahlstrom, *A Religious History of the American People* (Yale 1972); Owen Chadwick, *The Popes and the European Revolution* (on the eighteenth-century Catholic Church, OUP 1981), and *The Secularization of the European Mind in the Nineteenth Century* (CUP 1975); A. Hastings, *A History of African Christianity 1950–75* (CUP 1979); W. R. Hutchison, *The Modernist Impulse in American Protestantism* Harvard 1976); J. Macquarrie, *Twentieth-Century Religious Thought*)

(SCM Press 1963); M. Marty, *Protestantism* (Weidenfeld and Nicolson 1972); B. M. G. Reardon, *Liberal Protestantism* (a reader, A. & C. Black 1968), and *Liberalism and Tradition, Aspects of Catholic Thought in 19th-Century France* (CUP 1975); C. Welch, *Protestant Thought in the Nineteenth Century 1799–1870* (Yale 1972). On theology and science, M. Mandelbaum, *History, Man and Reason, a Study in Nineteenth-century Thought* (John Hopkins 1971); J. R. Moore, *The Post-Darwinian Controversies 1870–1900* (CUP 1979); A. R. Peacocke, *Creation and the World of Science* (OUP 1979); H. W. Paul, *The Edge of Contingency, French Catholic Reaction to Darwin* (Gainesville, Florida 1979) – and a fascinating book from the past, E. Boutroux, *Science and Religion in Contemporary Philosophy* (1909). On recent political theology: James H. Cone, *God of the Oppressed* (SPCK 1977); A. Fierro, *The Militant Gospel* (SCM Press 1977); A. Kee (ed), *Reader in Political Theology* (SCM Press 1974).

Since 1945 Anglo-Saxon theology has suffered from the decline of German Protestant theology, which is still absorbing recent German historical experience. In Britain, theology has been dominated by the linguistic and christological controversies which were summed up in J. Hick (ed), *The Myth of God Incarnate* (SCM Press 1979); more important was the relationship between Christianity and other religions: J. Hick, *God and the Universe of Faiths* (Macmillan 1973); D. Cupitt, *Taking Leave of God* SCM Press 1980).

Index of Names